VARGAS

VARGAS

By Alberto Vargas and Reid Austin

Foreword by Hugh Hefner

Harmony Books New York

*For Anna Mae Clift,
his gentle Ana,
who while retaining her
own identity became as
one with her husband*

Harmony Books, *a division of Crown Publishers, Inc.
One Park Avenue
New York, New York 10016*

*Published simultaneously in Canada by General Publishing
Company Limited.
Printed in Japan by Dai Nippon Printing Co., Ltd., Tokyo.*

Library of Congress Cataloging in Publication Data

*Austin, Reid.
Alberto Vargas.*

*1. Vargas, Alberto.   I. Vargas, Alberto, joint author.
ND1839.V35A96   759.13   77-3274
ISBN 0-517-530473   ISBN 0-517-530481 pbk.*

*Special Research Assistance by James Camperos
Photography by Jay Silverman
Book Design by Jean-Claude Suarés
assisted by Susan Willmarth*

PREFACE

It is probably a matter for discussion, since most things of any importance are, but while preparing this volume it became increasingly obvious to me that the pungency of Alberto Vargas' work aside, he is assuredly one of the finest watercolorists the United States ever sheltered, and the world's most accessible and popular surrealist. Alberto wouldn't approve of the latter appellation, for, interestingly, he considers himself a realist.

By any accepted definition, he is not a realist. He is a surrealist, as the majority of pieces reproduced here emphatically testify. Any of the portraits, for example, shout down realism. Idealism, yes. Realism, no. His work at its best certainly contains fantastic, dreamlike qualities which slide idealism surreptitiously into surreality. Alberto would find all of this rather academic. He only knows that he must paint beautiful women, come hell or high water. His dream has been to immortalize the American Girl, and he has done this beyond any question, and done it better than anyone else.

Considering how greatly Vargas has influenced artists and certainly photographers, it is interesting that no one has been able to successfully copy, or even satirize, his style. His technique is a tenacious phenomenon that will perhaps die with him, for there are few, if any, young men ready to tackle a technique of which the foremost ingredient is patience. Ours is a quick, quicker age. Airbrushing used as the end rather than the means suits such an age.

At his best he brings elegance, insouciance, innocence, and honesty to a unique field more often than not marked by questionable taste and mayonnaise craftsmanship, thereby raising it to its most aesthetically respectable level.

One would hope in this television-ridden age, an age of Sonny and Cher's divorce, of automatism by Diet Cola, of global unity by McDonald's, of hyperfrivolity and anxiety that makes most past self-indulgence seem heavy-handed indeed, that apologies aren't necessary in order to admit Alberto Vargas to a strong position among those artists who share sincere dedication, singular drive, and devotion to one goal—to paint a picture that makes them happy and has meaning for others beyond the lifetime of its creator.

Do what thy manhood bids thee do,
From none but self expect applause;
He noblest lives and noblest dies who
Makes and keeps his self-made laws.

–Sir Richard Francis Burton
The Kasidah of Haji Abdu El Yazdi

"The Kimono Girl," a
Ziegfeld poster posed
by Kathlyn Martyn,
1922, approx. 28″ x
40″.

Contents

FOREWORD

I remember my first meeting with Alberto Vargas. It was back in 1956 when *Playboy* was still in its embryonic years, being published rather modestly out of the old Playboy Building on Chicago's East Ohio Street. Vargas had been one of the major reasons for *Esquire*'s tremendous success in the forties. His leggy, pulchritudinous creations, drawn under the name "Varga", had gamboled and lolled in seductive innocence from month to month, reminding the boys overseas that there was more at home than just mom's apple pie.

But those days were behind Vargas; they had ended in costly litigation with the magazine that had left him and his beloved wife Anna Mae, a former Follies beauty, emotionally as well as financially drained. There was no hint of this in our meeting, however. The Vargases had flown to Chicago to show me a collection of never-before-published large nudes that Alberto had been working on since the early 1940s. As soon as he removed the first one from its covering I had the feeling that something lasting was about to begin. The work was exquisite. Despite our then-limited budget, we ran six of the best drawings in our March 1957 issue. Reader response was very encouraging. One reader even wrote requesting that we run a Vargas girl monthly on the flip-side of our gatefold. I then decided to begin publishing Vargas's work on a regular basis. It's a decision I've never had cause to regret.

I think it was in 1963 that I visited the Vargases at their Westwood home one afternoon. I intended it to be a very brief visit since my West Coast trip was jammed with business commitments.

Shortly after I arrived, Alberto invited me to see his studio. Once inside he began a fascinating set of reminiscences about his days with Ziegfeld and *Esquire* which he punctuated with a parade of paintings he had done during those years.

When it became apparent that the visit wouldn't be brief, Anna Mae produced an impromptu lunch of avocado-and-bacon sandwiches and iced coffee, apologizing for their lack of Pepsi Cola. Night had long since fallen by the time I left them. I had had to cancel a number of appointments, but that suddenly seemed very unimportant. I had unexpectedly experienced Alberto Vargas's unquenchable enthusiasm for his art in spite of the numerous obstacles he had faced. Those hours will remain indelible in my memory.

HUGH M. HEFNER

"Art Deco Dietrich,"
(opposite page)
painted for the
Paramount Studios
yearbook, 1931.

"La Familia de Max
Vargas," 1906.
*Front row, seated
left to right:* George,
Fred, Max, and
Alice. *Standing:*
Alberto, Margarita,
Max, Jr. and Laura.

An exquisitely de-
tailed pen-and-ink
done in 1915 by
nineteen-year-old
Alberto. Preoccupa-
tion with detail and
texture can readily
be seen.

A MAN AND HIS WOMAN

High in the mountains of Peru, about five hundred miles
southeast of Lima, lies the city of Arequipa. An eagle's
nest, it spreads out white and glistening in a broad valley
guarded by three none-too-benign volcanoes. Arequipa
was, and is still today, Peru's second-largest city; the
faces of its inhabitants reflecting their proud Inca ances-
tors, with a slight nod to the Spanish conquerors.

Joaquin Alberto Vargas y Chavez was born into this
rarefied atmosphere on February 9, 1896. The firstborn
son of a practical and indulgent Margarita Vargas, Alberto was reared with the certitude that he would enter
his father's business and assume its responsibilities.

Max Vargas was a very successful photographer, with
studios in Arequipa and La Paz, Bolivia. A perfectionist
much sought after by peasant and politician alike for his
portraits, he also had an excellent reputation for land-
scapes, his photographic studies of the town of Cuzco
winning, in 1911, a gold medal in Paris. This was all
rather sophisticated for a remote colonial town in Peru.
The young, imaginative Alberto grew and thrived in the
heady atmosphere of his father's studio.

One day when his father ordered him into a corner as
penance for some mischief, the boy asked for something
to keep himself amused. His busy father thrust at him
crayons and paper and at that moment a passion began
that would grow to control his entire life. He began
spending his free time with his father, learning all there
was to learn about photography, even retouching delicate photograph negative plates and photo enlargements
using the relatively new and cumbersome airbrush, a tool
that enables the artist, by means of compressed air and
deft control, to spray a very fine mist of liquid color.

Margarita had long ago determined that her sons were
to receive the best education possible, the education she
and her husband had been denied, and that unquestion-
ably meant the ateliers of Europe. Thus, in 1911, Alberto
and his younger brother, Max Jr., were off to Switzerland in the company of Papa, who would pick up his gold
medal, conduct some business, and see the boys settled
in their respective schools. Arrangements were made for
Alberto's eventual apprenticeship with Julien Studios in
Geneva and Sarony Court Photographers in London,
while his brother was to study banking and finance in
Geneva.

Before journeying on to Switzerland, the two boys had
time to explore Paris while their father conducted business there. For Alberto, the museums and galleries
offered a veritable feast for the eye. Never had he sus-

pected that such things existed, and he quickly singled out Ingres as one of his favorite painters, spending hours examining and copying his work. Ingres' elegant world of flesh and fabric hypnotized the sensitive young Latin.

On the streets of Paris he was exposed to another quite different form of artistic expression: the women of *La Vie Parisiènne*. He found the saucy drawings that filled this popular magazine eye-opening. Raphael Kirchner became the boy's idol. Kirchner's elegant and limpid beauties were rendered in the softest watercolors with never a hint of bad taste. Kirchner's reputation was such that in 1916 the great Florenz Ziegfeld commissioned him to do a number of large lobby paintings for his *Follies*. (Five of these paintings can still be seen at the rear orchestra section of New York's Winter Garden Theatre.)

Alberto spent the next few years in Rappersville, a suburb of Zurich, studying. He read voraciously, developing a rather radical streak which can boil to the surface even today, as can his polyglot mastery of French and German.

In 1915 he went to Geneva to begin his apprenticeship with Monsieur Julien. This was interrupted in early 1916 by a cable from the senior Vargas instructing him to leave for England immediately to assume his position with Sarony. When Alberto arrived in Paris he found he couldn't get to England because of wartime restrictions. Sarony politely informed him by letter that they needed him now, not later, and French officials advised him to return to Switzerland until the situation cleared.

With Europe erupting around him, Alberto discovered that ships were still sailing for America and, considering discretion the better part of valor, he booked passage for New York with an eventual connection to Peru. His father was so advised. Max, Jr. would join his brother in New York as soon as possible.

In October of 1916 Alberto hit New York—we should say New York hit him! Leaving the ship, he trudged up Fourteenth Street amid clang, clunk, rumble, and chug of trolley, El, and auto. As he met Broadway the clock struck noon. "From every building came torrents of girls. . . . I had never seen anything like it. . . . Hundreds of girls with an air of self-assuredness and determination that said, 'Here I am, how do you like me?' This certainly was not the Spanish, Swiss, or French girl!" He fell head over heels for "Las Gringas" and became enthralled with the raucous beauty of New York City.

Within a few days he knew he couldn't return to Peru. This new world was too exciting. He also knew that his father expected him on the next boat and that some plan must be made to avoid a future in Arequipa.

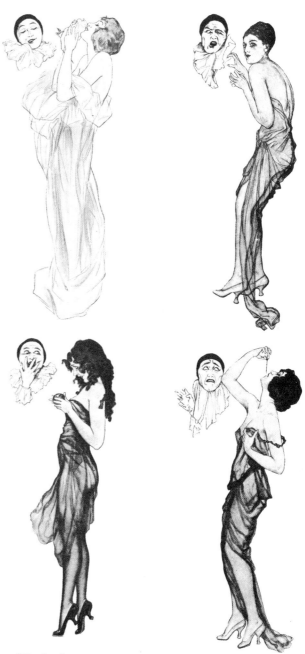

Four of Raphael Kirchner's "Seven Deadly Sins" painted in 1916 for Florenz Ziegfeld's *Follies*. The surviving panels from this series now hang in the Winter Garden Theatre in New York.

*Greenwich Village
Follies* beauty Anna
Mae Clift strikes a
statuesque pose,
circa 1921.

Anna Mae takes the
cake, or rather deco-
rates it, as one of four
candles in the "Just
Sweet Sixteen" pro-
duction number from
the *G.V.F.* 1920 edi-
tion.

The arrival of his brother, Max, who was to work in a New York bank, forced Alberto's hand. In an uncharacteristic and desperate move he told Max that a cable had been received from their father ordering Max home to assume his place in the studio; Alberto was to stay in New York. Max fell for it, to Alberto's astonished relief. He had now only to await the admonition of his duped father.

Señor Vargas calmly informed his son that since he had made this decision to find his own way in a new land, he could no longer expect financial support, but should accept everyone's best wishes for his success.

Alberto, filled with the to-hell-with-everything attitude of youth, immediately got a job retouching negatives for a Fifth Avenue photographer; but after seven months he quit, dissatisfied with such a closeted existence. His first job involving artwork was with Butterick Patterns, where he drew hats and heads while other artists did shoes and legs. He had noticed that "every magazine cover except National Geographic had a painting of a pretty girl." This was the age of Gibson, Nell Brinkley, Penrhyn Stanlaws, Harrison Fisher, Neysa McMein, Coles Phillips, and Leyendecker, among others. With this group of glittering stars as his inspiration, he decided that he was going to become an artist. He had been working constantly in pen-and-ink and watercolors; Russell Flint, the great British watercolorist, particularly affected his technique. He now tried in earnest to master oils and pastels—any and every medium.

In late 1917 he sold his first freelance work: three pen-and-inks for five dollars each. Then five more at thirty dollars each. Encouraged, he quit Butterick and began getting enough jobs to support himself.

At about the same time, Alberto met a slender, strawberry-blonde beauty from Soddy, Tennessee: Anna Mae Clift. She was working as a show girl in John Murray Anderson's *Greenwich Village Follies*, rival to Florenz Ziegfeld's then staggeringly popular *Follies*. Anna Mae was a particular favorite of Anderson's for, in addition to her ability to take direction well, he found her Southern accent and abundant hair irresistible. To augment her earnings, she worked days as a haute couture mannequin in Seventh Avenue's garment district.

The young man was instantly attracted by her vivaciousness and warmth, but his poor English and mid-Victorian manners precluded any attempt at communicating his confused feelings. It would in fact be six years before he ceased calling her Miss Clift. He recalls that when, in Latin tradition, he would kiss a lady's hand, often American friends would comment critically. His reply to this: "Lo cortez, no quita lo valiente."

("Courtesy does not diminish manhood.")

Though Miss Clift worked odd hours she would make every effort, when asked, to pose for the "Little Artist," never charging him and lightly brushing away his efforts to pay her.

In the interim Alberto's preoccupation with watercolor became evident. His use of this medium increased and he began achieving particularly unusual effects, a softness and smoothness unlike that of anyone else. His facility with the airbrush meant that he could, if he wished, use it for a final touch of silkiness. Also, by 1919 he was concentrating almost exclusively on paintings of girls, his style heavily influenced by the French manner of Maurice Millière and Kirchner.

In late May of that year, a friend who knew of his talent for painting girls persuaded him to take a job as part of a window display promotion in the Corona Typewriter Building. Dressed in smock and beret, he was to paint a girl draped in a Spanish shawl. In the background would be a group of his paintings. Alberto's nature rejected the scheme but he allowed himself to be convinced. It was murderously hot in the window and Alberto found it a generally mortifying experience made bearable only by keeping his back to the crowds that filled the sidewalk. He agreed to do this for a week and was encouraged by the notes and letters he received regarding his paintings.

On the fifth day, Sam Kingston, general manager for Florenz Ziegfeld, left his card requesting that Vargas bring his samples to Ziegfeld's office the following day. Oh, New York. Oh, dreams of glory.

Florenz Ziegfeld's *Follies* were the most splendidly produced, price-is-no-object spectacles ever seen on Broadway and have been equaled only by MGM and the Grand Canyon. Ziegfeld was to women what Christ was to the apostles. His glorification of his women (and himself) was such that one would think he had invented them, and to a real extent he had—the Show Girl was decidedly his creation.

His *Follies*, begun in 1907, had steadily increased in popularity and splendor. The 1918 edition had proved to be an unsurpassed hit with critics and public alike.

Having reached this pinnacle, Ziegfeld determined that the 1919 edition would be better than its predecessor. All the stops were out. The stars were Marilyn Miller, who with this production would become a cult star, Eddie Dowling, Ray Dooley, Eddie Cantor, Van & Schenk, and Bert Williams, whose big song was "You Cannot Make Your Shimmy Shake on Tea." John Steele sang another of the many hits Irving Berlin had provided

Coy, voluptuous, and very French. This hoyden, painted in 1916 by Maurice Millière, exhibits every texture young Alberto was most fascinated by. Paintings such as this greatly influenced his work.

"Indiscrete Leaves" was pretty daring stuff sixty years ago.

A rather elfin portrait of elfin Billie Burke Ziegfeld, painted for the boss in 1920.

for the score, "A Pretty Girl Is Like a Melody," which suited the "Ziegfeld Walk" to perfection. This, according to revue authority Robert Baral, combined "Irene Castle's flair for accenting the pelvis, the lifted shoulder and a slow, concentrated gait. A girl would enter the spotlight very quietly—no smile visible. As she proceeded downstage a glimmer would appear. . . . As she reached center stage she'd turn her full allure on the audience." It was a killer.

Alberto remembers his first visit to the great Ziegfeld very well. The producer immediately opened a closet filled with paintings of *Follies* stars and show girls. Among the group were some by Raphael Kirchner. When asked if he thought he could do such work, Alberto explained in his best English that Kirchner had been his idol and he could only try his best. Ziegfeld insisted that Alberto could do it, and said he would pay him two hundred dollars per painting in return for having first call on the artist's services. So a twelve-year relationship began with a simple handshake.

The producer made it clear that vulgarity had no place in a Ziegfeld production; there could be no blatant nudity in the paintings. Sex should be implicit, only alluded to.

The paintings commissioned were to be placed all over the lobby walls of the New Amsterdam Theatre, so Alberto decided that thirty-by-forty-inch watercolor boards would have to be used if they were to be seen.

Ziegfeld arranged for stars and show girls to make themselves available for appointments at Alberto's fifth floor walk-up studio, where he worked frantically to finish the twenty or so portraits ordered—among them, one of Marilyn Miller in a tutu, pertly perched atop a tall stool.

The last painting was finished only hours before the June 16 opening, which rocked Broadway. The 1919 edition was simply perfection.

Alberto usually painted twelve or more portraits for each edition of the *Follies*. A partial list of some of the stars and show girls painted includes: Fanny Brice, Dolores, Eddie Cantor, W. C. Fields, Marilyn Miller, Ann Pennington, Olive Thomas, Gladys Glad, Hazel Forbes, Anastasia Reilly, Hilda Ferguson, Mary Eaton, Paulette Goddard, Claire Luce, Peggy Fears, Jessie Reed, Mae Murray, Justine Johnstone, Gilda Gray, Vivienne Segal, Caja Erick, Cynthia Cambridge, Nita Naldi, Shirley Vernon, Ray Dooley, Kathlyn Martyn, Ruth Etting, Greta Nissen, and Ina Claire. He also painted portraits of the principals for all of Ziegfeld's side productions, including the immortal *Show Boat*.

Alberto explains that, though time would seem to have

been plentiful for the production of these annual paintings, in actual fact the contrary was true. The girls chosen had to first be fitted, worked on by makeup people, hairdressers, photographers, and so on. He would get them last. This perfunctory note from Ziegfeld gives some idea of the time allotted Alberto. His ability to work carefully and swiftly under pressure was to be tested many times in his life.

July 9, 1926

Miss Nissen
Miss Brown
Miss Fears
Miss Dooley
Miss Newberry
Miss Luce
Miss Leedom

to have portraits painted by Mr. A. Vargas
work to be finished by July 19, 1926

F. Ziegfeld

The period from 1920 to 1929 was a very busy one for Alberto. With his Ziegfeld work came many assignments, among them a commission from the *New York Tribune* for a series of full-page Nell Brinkleyish ink-and-watercolor nursery-rhyme illustrations; an exquisite series of figure studies and portraits for *Shadowland*, an elegant arts magazine, in then rare color; a similar commission from Hearst's *American Weekly;* covers for *Motion Picture* magazine; advertisements, sheet music covers, brochures, and personal commissions for portraits.

All of this work should have brought him considerable money, and it did bring some, but it only meant that he could buy all the books he desired. Books were a weakness: art, philosophy, poetry, he loved all of them. Clothes, too, were important. Early photos show an immaculately groomed dandy of the Valentino variety. He spent most of his time painting: if not for a client, then for his own pleasure and experiment—specifically, nudes of some of the show girls who posed for him. If one of the girls asked him to paint her portrait, he would, at no charge. If a friend admired a painting, he would give it to him. This explains why so much of his work from the 1920s has vanished. His relaxation came from painting, his books, and evenings spent with artist and writer friends.

He simply had no understanding of or regard for money. He was comfortable and happy; that was enough. A very good example of his complacency and compliance where his work and its worth were concerned can be found in this letter from S. Davies Warfield, then president of Seaboard Railway Company, relating to a poster

A beautifully agitated Art Nouveau portrait of Norma Talmadge created in 1919.

Alberto surrounded by some unfinished business. Since the paintings shown are nudes they weren't meant for Ziegfeld who allowed no overt nudity. Breast clutching was fine, but no nipples.

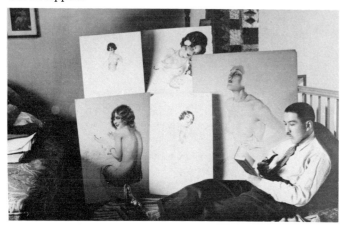

Painted for the *Follies*, this portrait of showgirl Beryl Halley also adorned the sheet music for the 1924 edition's only hit song," Adoring You."

for which Ina Claire had posed:

> Baltimore, Md., May 28th, 1925
> (At New York)
>
> Mr. Albert Vargas,
>   109 West Forty-eight Street,
>   New York
> Dear Mr. Vargas:
>   I have not had the opportunity of seeing you in respect to the "Orange Blossom Girl" portrait which you painted and which was a decided success. This picture, of course, the Seaboard Air Line Railway wishes to use exclusively, since it is, as you may well understand, a trade mark and we would not wish it used in any other direction.
>   In this connection, while you were kind enough to say that you would not expect to make any charge for the admirable work you did and Mr. Ziegfeld was good enough to state that he would be glad to have you do this for us, I take pleasure in handing you herewith check for $500 which I hope you will accept with the compliments of the Seaboard Air Line Railway.
>
>   Very truly yours,
>   S. Davies Warfield [signature]
>   President.

During this time "Miss Clift" continued posing for Alberto whenever he desired, still refusing payment. Her personal life was unhappy and confused. Coming from a poor background and a broken home, she had hoped to find much-needed security in New York. Her search led her to the cliché of bright lights, jazz, all-night parties, and drinking that has come to represent the 1920s. She didn't like what she found. On the other hand, she found "her artist" kind, intelligent, handsome, a perfect gentleman, and maddeningly impractical—a Bohemian, if you will. He represented the antithesis of what she needed. She knew that Alberto was in love with her and also realized that, against her better judgment, she could fall in love with him.

He found her choice of companions, her late hours, and her gay life irritating, but above all he knew that he loved her although he couldn't understand her.

She stubbornly resisted any change in her goals and life-style to suit Alberto Vargas. Equally stubborn, he remained staunch in his views. Détente was the modus operandi from the mid-twenties until 1929.

Anna Mae's then current beau surprised her with a proposal. Her dream had come true. Within days, however, she realized that she didn't want the dream—she wanted Alberto. Despite nagging friends and her own lingering misgivings, she declared her love to the only man who made her feel important, needed, and loved—the only man she had ever fully trusted.

A sensitively
sketched Swedish
beauty who danced in
the *Follies*, circa
1928.

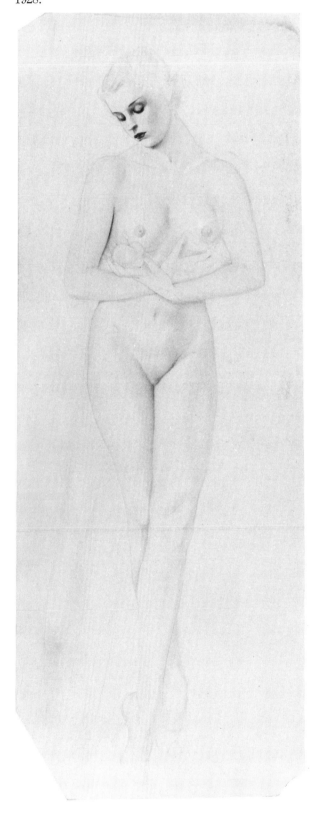

Once aware of each other's devotion, the two lost no time in cementing the relationship. Anna Mae moved into Alberto's studio and began a long attempt to bring stability to his financially chaotic life.

Louis Sobil's July 23, 1930 column in the *New York Graphic* announced: "Albert Vargas, noted society artist, and Anna Mae Clift, famous model, eloped a month ago." They were married on June 9, 1930—Alberto had to borrow the money for the license.

Changing theatrical styles, ill health, and a crumbling stock market wrote *fini* to Ziegfeld's glittering star. The 1931 *Follies* was the last personally produced edition. This unhappy event and changing art styles forced Alberto to retrench. He found little market for his Ziegfeld-style girls. As the Depression grew darker, so did Vargas' financial picture.

As early as 1926 he had begun using pastel for some of his portrait commissions, posters, and magazine covers. Although a number of these pastels are exceptional, the majority exhibit a lack of involvement if not of interest on Alberto's part. These and fashion illustrations, styled in the French mode, became his main endeavors. One of the portrait commissions he obtained was reported by Walter Winchell on April 5, 1932: "Alberto Vargas, the better portraiter, can't get Tony Biddle to sit long enough to complete the picture." Anna Mae continued her modeling, which helped support the couple while Alberto searched for work. Among other things he did a number of covers for *Theatre*, *Tatler*, and *Dance* magazines, some counter display pastel illustrations for Old Gold cigarettes, and a series of hairstyle illustrations for *Harper's Bazaar*, for which he received fifty dollars apiece. He even got an agency job repainting or translating John LaGatta paintings into color; LaGatta had difficulty working in color, so the agency had various artists redo his black and white work. In sum, Alberto did a great deal and made little.

Probably the most significant work of this period is a series of full-length movie star portraits commissioned by Hellmann's mayonnaise in 1934—significant in that they so thoroughly break with the "Parisienne" influence of the 1920s and bear such remarkable resemblance to the work he would do within seven years for *Esquire* magazine.

Nothing he had done prior to this prepares us for the simple directness of the figures, worked fully and masterfully in his forte, watercolor. These pieces unfortunately carried no signature when reproduced. The softness of newspaper reproduction also eliminated most of the delicate technique, so that even a knowledgeable eye

Watercolor study,
circa 1920, approx.
12″ x 17″.

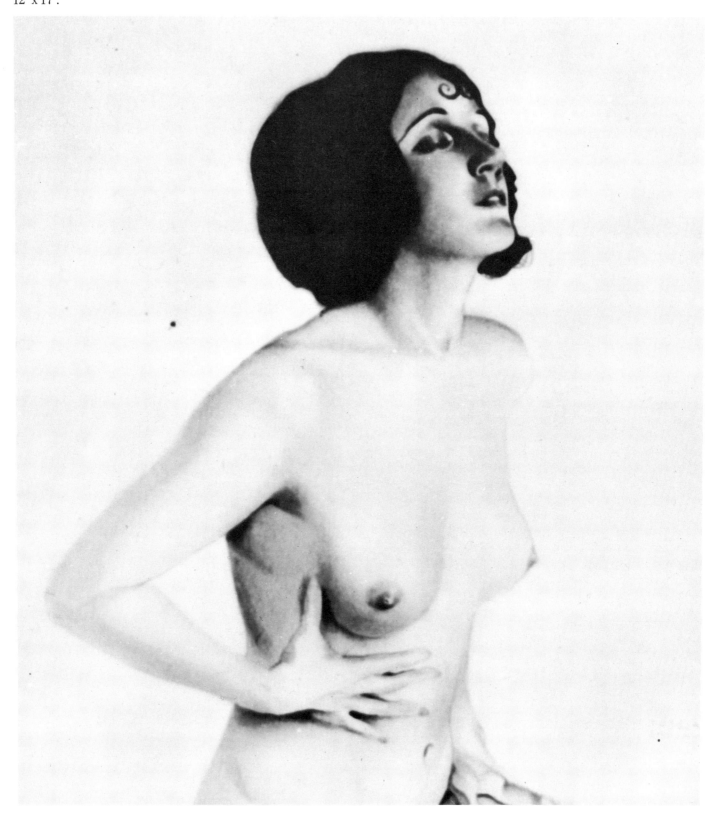

Untitled, circa 1920,
approx. 20″ x 30″.

Anna Mae Vargas poses dreamily before the couple's first and only home. Though altered somewhat, the Westwood bungalow remains the modest structure it was in 1936.

would tend to assume they were photographs.

Though portents of a career undreamed of, these salad-dressing girls did not affect Vargas' future as much as did the motion picture ad work he began about 1930.

The major studios all had their advertising offices in New York, and Alberto found them eager for sexually implicit images of their stars. Most of this work was for Paramount. The most interesting piece was for a forgotten Miriam Hopkins epic called *Song of Songs*, a ". . . story of a spoiled girl too weak to grasp true happiness." The painting had been done by Alberto in 1920 and the model was nude.

The art director liked it and asked Alberto to cover up the figure with a full slip, which he did. Alberto had consented to sell it provided he got the original back. When he got it back he proceeded to raise the hemline of the slip to chemise proportions.*

Hollywood! Toward the end of 1934, just when the Vargases had begun to lose all hope of ever connecting with a major advertising account, a call came from Winfield Sheehan, then head of the Fox movie studio. Having been impressed by Alberto's work for Paramount, he convinced him to come to Hollywood and do a number of pastel portraits of Fox stars at two hundred dollars each. With one-way fares provided by Fox, the Vargases boarded the 20th Century Limited filled with hope and confidence. When Alberto had finished his assigned portraits, Sheehan prevailed upon him to remain at Fox and work in their art department. He was essentially starting at the bottom, for though Sheehan's presence made things easier than they might have been, he was still exposed to an artistic environment totally foreign to anything he had experienced. The one work remaining from this association is an oil portrait honoring Shirley Temple, which can still be seen in the Fox commissary.

Within a few months a hurricane named Zanuck blew in as the new head of Fox, and Vargas was blown out along with Sheehan. Anna Mae, determined that they weren't going to start hand-to-mouthing it again, called her good friend from the *Follies* days, Busby Berkeley, choreographic wizard-in-residence at Warner's.

Berkeley was the darling of the Warner Brothers lot and within days he had a job for Alberto in their design department. Alberto worked under Warner's head art director, Anton Grott. The two men became friends: Alberto credits Grott with teaching him much and teaching him well. His tenure at Warner's was lengthy, as these

---

*This painting eventually found its way into *Playboy*'s lengthy 1964 takeout, "The Vargas Girl, circa 1920."

things go. Actually, to try to give a chronology of his jobs at various studios would be impossible. Suffice it to say that he worked for every major studio, and for some of them more than once.

His best work was done for Warner's; his elevations or visuals for *Juarez* are gems of light, shadow, and composition—a far cry from his first love, girls, but very successful and illuminating, nonetheless.

The Vargases had lived in numerous rooming houses in the area since their arrival. Tired of this and feeling a deep need for roots, in 1936 they put a down payment on a small bungalow in Westwood, surrounded by walnut groves. This was a very happy period for them. They were in their first home, they had a garden that Alberto doted on, the "kids" (a pair of wirehaired terrier puppies, Poocho and Jitters), and a small studio where Alberto went every evening to perfect "his girl."

Although his drawings still reflected the somewhat stilted "dying swan" attitudes of the 1920s, his water-color technique was undergoing considerable change. His earlier works, usually on tinted boards, consisted entirely of medium tones with few highlights and little shadowing. Perhaps due to his new studio conditions, and certainly due to his use of white boards, his flesh tones now acquired a translucent silky sheen with great depth. We see numerous tones blended to produce an uncanny reality. His color became firmer, less ethereal.

When his co-workers discovered that Alberto spent his evenings painting girls, he regularly received ribbing about it, including constant inquiry as to what he thought of George Petty's latest cartoon in *Esquire*. Once, in a fit of typical Vargas bravado, he told them that he could easily get Petty's job if he wished to. That silenced no one, and the irritating gibes went on.

In September of 1939 Alberto joined a minority of his fellow studio artists in a unionization walkout. As a result he was blackballed and soon found that all studio doors had clanged shut with resounding finality. For eight empty months no money came in. Through the generosity of friends, by taking in boarders, and by borrowing on their insurance policies the Vargases had scraped through so far, but the situation could not continue.

Back against the wall, a desperate Anna Mae finally convinced her *very* reluctant husband to return to New York and attempt to reestablish former contacts in the advertising field. Hunger knows no master: portfolio in hand and one suit to his name, Alberto bussed back to Manhattan in May 1940.

The pickings were slim for a desperate and out-of-touch artist. He had only obtained a few small poster jobs

Alberto did a number of portraits of Fox's animated little gold mine Shirley Temple, and portraits of all the studio's stars as well, during his brief tenure there in 1934.

"California Gold and Aztec Gold": two set designs produced while employed by Warner Brothers, circa 1938.

from the Warner Brothers office in New York and had gotten a nibble of interest from the agency handling Jantzen swim suits, when a friend looked at Alberto's samples and urged him, as a number of others had, to go to *Esquire;* he had heard that Petty was out and they were looking for someone. Alberto refused, saying he was sure he had nothing for them. Actually he was terrified of rejection, having bragged that he could get Petty's job. In truth he did think he was better than Petty, but couldn't admit that inner confidence. The friend then made an appointment for Alberto to see a Mr. Kaufman. When Alberto stepped off the elevator at Kaufman's office, he found it was actually the secretaried vestibule of *Esquire*'s offices. Confronted so suddenly with the need to make a decision, he went in. Kaufman seemed very interested and left the room, returning with *Esquire*'s New York chief, Sidney Carroll. After openly discussing the need for an artist who "could out-Petty Petty," Carroll made a hurried call to *Esquire*'s home office in Chicago. Returning, he said that the home office wanted to see Vargas' things. Could Alberto leave them? Alberto said that he couldn't, since he would need them to show as samples, but consented to leave one particular painting. Alberto had little hope of anything materializing as the weeks went by.

Husband and wife wrote each other religiously. Their letters of this period give a vivid picture of the love between them. Each tries to put up a front brimming with hope and support:

> Letter of May 6, 1940, after Anna Mae hears that he has made a contact with Jantzen. "Your drawings need more smile and movement. . . . They all are really gorgeous, but in that commercial field it is not real art that counts, but splash!"

> Letter of May 18: Anna Mae tells Alberto he has been blacklisted as a Communist because of his position during the strike and warns against radical talk with strangers. She reminds him, "We are idealists and that doesn't work in a streamlined age."

At one point in early June, Anna Mae gives in to an overwhelming despair, dangerously close to a breakdown. The burden of bills, mortgage, boarders, and worry about Alberto in New York has become more than she can take. Alberto, summoning every ounce of strength, demands, then begs her to be strong for *their* sake, assuring her that something will break for him.

Within the week the magic began.

On June 12 he got a call from Carroll. Could he come over the next day?

Due to Carroll's enthusiasm and certain qualities in the

Three dramatic elevations done by Alberto for Warner's *Juarez* in 1938. He worked on many of their most celebrated films, including *The Sea Hawk* and *Elizabeth and Essex.*

sample sent to Chicago, *Esquire*'s owner-publisher, David Smart, had made a special trip to New York to see Alberto personally.

David Smart was a forty-eight-year-old grand panjandrum: dapper, fastidious to a fault (he wouldn't touch door handles in public conveyances without first wiping them clean with his handkerchief), enthusiastic, and shrewd. He had many interests; one in particular was a proprietary concern in *Esquire*'s artists and cartoonists that bordered on the feudal.

George Petty, originally a photo-retoucher just beginning to gain a bit of Midwestern prominence as a poster artist, had been discovered by Arnold Gingrich, Smart's invaluable, ultraliterate editor-in-chief, during the planning stage of the first issue of the magazine. Petty appeared regularly, if erratically, from that first issue, in autumn of 1933, until April of 1940. With one exception, his work appeared as a single page "cartoon." The double fold-out (gatefold) concept wasn't initiated by *Esquire* until the December 1939 issue, which contained four of them, one of which was a Petty Girl.

Initially Petty worked from the dozens of rough ideas sketched by the fabulous and fecund black cartoonist E. Simms Campbell, another Gingrich discovery. These first cartoons featured a fat, bald, bulbous-eyed gentleman of advanced years confronting a Harlowesque blond. Within eighteen months the gent had vanished and soon all background and props also vanished, leaving only the girl, who carried a telephone with its umbilical cord to the outside world: a David Smart conceit to facilitate editorial gag lines.

Petty had no contract with *Esquire*. He made about a hundred dollars per picture in 1933; by 1939, he was making about a thousand.

As an artist, Petty was a brilliant businessman. According to Gingrich, "George was the original tightwad." Through the singular popularity of his *Esquire* pictures he had obtained two enormous advertising contracts—Old Gold cigarettes and Jantzen swimwear—in addition to many smaller accounts. His work for *Esquire* was sketchy and incomplete compared with his beautifully realized ad work, probably due to two facts: he received absolutely no art direction at *Esquire* and his ad accounts were far more lucrative.

Throughout the late 1930s Petty became increasingly hard to handle. Besides demanding more money, he insisted that his originals be returned to him. He was a bear of a man who preferred hunting and fishing to painting. Smart couldn't stand dealing with him on a personal basis. To quote Gingrich: "George wasn't subservient

George Petty's Girl in action for Jantzen Swimsuits, circa 1937. This was only one of many significant Petty advertising accounts.

The inscription on this photo of David Smart reads: "To my talented friends Al Vargas and his good wife Anna Mae who labor like slaves to perpetuate the Zieg-feld tradition so that *Esquire* can boast 'Through these pages walk (and lie) the most beautiful girls in the world.' Sincerely, David A. Smart 7/16/42"

enough for Dave." Smart left Gingrich the task of handling the rebellious artist. If a particularly sketchy finish came in, it was known that "George is pouting again."

Petty's demands became awesome by the end of 1939. He refused to work without a strong contract in his favor. Smart again sent Gingrich into the bear's den.

An agreement was reached by mid-1940 that shows how far Gingrich would go in order to reinstate the Petty Girl, which had been missing from the magazine since the April issue. On the basis of a one-year contract running from January through December of 1941, Petty was to do twelve paintings at fifteen hundred dollars each. *Esquire* would retain permanent ownership of the paintings, but the artist retained any and all reprint rights he wished. The paintings could be "borrowed" at any time and then returned to *Esquire*. They were borrowed often, flopped, restyled, recostumed, and rehashed.

Additionally, a "Petty Date Book" and glossy, framed reprints of each month's gatefold to be offered for sale through the magazine were dreamed up as further "sops" to the artist. The profits from these sops would, of course, be split equitably.

Smart's money problem with George Petty caused him much trouble at a time when he needed Petty most and trouble least. *Esquire*'s circulation had taken a plunge in the 1938 recession from which it was still recovering, and it was evident to all that the general outbreak of a world war was only a matter of time. Smart desperately needed a "girl" for *Esquire*, and a quiet search for replacement had led nowhere. He knew what he wanted and until this moment he had held little hope of finding it. Discovering an artist who used a watercolor and airbrush technique almost identical to and better than Petty's seemed the impossible come true.

Qualities unique to the Petty Girl by 1941 were big legs, smiling redundant faces, and action. The artist's peculiar stylization gave even reflective, quiet poses a taut aura of frozen tension. Tangents abounded. She was designed as a Maserati is designed. Anomalous anatomical abberations produced a streamlined, enameled equivocation of life.

Alberto's creation was, by comparison, trompe l'oeil. One foolishly believed she could exist. Even in action she and her linear composition remained relaxed and utterly feminine. (She even flew with aplomb. The December 1943 gatefold would find her floating naïvely and happily through space garbed in red, white, and blue chiffon, in a pose that would make an Olympic gymnast blanch.)

After going over the Vargas samples, Smart asked about the artist's background. Alberto told of his career and openly discussed his recent problems, his devoted wife who waited in California, and his difficulties in getting established in New York. Such diffidence suited Smart perfectly.

Smart calmly asked if Alberto would be interested in signing a contract with *Esquire*. If so, it would mean coming to Chicago, since it would be important for him to work closely with Smart to ensure that Alberto met the necessary requirements. Alberto averred that he would be very willing to try such an arrangement since Mr. Smart had so much confidence in him. In his letter of June 13 he announces to an astonished Anna Mae: "He told me all about this [about Petty] for he said it was an unpleasant experience all around and he wanted to see how I measure up to the chance. In other words he wants to *make me* if I am willing to toe the mark and put myself in their hands *entirely*! Well, what would you have done? Well—I did it."

Smart, realizing Alberto's financial state, asked if he had money for train fare to Chicago. With typical bravado Alberto slapped his wallet, saying yes. Smart gave him the necessary money.

Within three hours of his arrival in Chicago, after an introductory meeting in Smart's office at which Arnold Gingrich was present, Alberto signed a contract. It is worth printing here in full.

1940 Contract

Memorandum of Agreement between Esquire, Inc., a Delaware corporation (hereinafter referred to as "Esquire"), party of the first part, and Alberto Vargas of Hollywood, California (hereinafter referred to as "Vargas"), party of the second part.

Witnesseth

Esquire is engaged directly or through subsidiary and affiliated companies, in the publication of the magazines "Esquire," "Coronet," "Apparel Arts," and may from time to time during the term of this agreement be engaged in the publication of other magazines and publications. Esquire also, directly or indirectly, is engaged in the business of supplying editorial and art material for various advertising and other commercial uses.

Vargas is an artist and desires to serve Esquire as an employe, and under such employment to furnish to Esquire such art material as he is able to produce which will be acceptable for use in the magazines published by Esquire during the term of this agreement and for use by Esquire in selling or otherwise exploiting the use of such art material produced by Vargas in such commercial ways as Esquire may approve. Esquire is willing to employ Vargas for these purposes and this agreement has been entered into to set forth the terms and conditions of the employment arrangements which have this

"and this, gentlemen, is what is technically termed a pin-up"

Esquire　A FAVORED MAGAZINE OF FIGHTING MEN

And this from a 1943 newspaper is one of the many ways in which *Esquire* promoted its most popular feature, The "Varga" Girl. "Varga" by-products included the "Varga" Calendar, postcards, playing cards, and advertising calendars.

This sanguine chalk
sketch was the basis
for the first "Varga"
Girl.

date been agreed upon between Esquire and Vargas.

Accordingly, in consideration of the mutual convenants and agreements hereinafter contained, It Is Agreed by and between Esquire and Vargas as follows, that is to say:

1. Esquire does hereby employ Vargas as an artist for the period of three years commencing on July 1, 1940.

2. During the term of said employment Vargas shall devote his entire time to the services of Esquire and shall diligently endeavor to produce such art work as he is able to produce and which will be acceptable for use in the publications published directly or indirectly by Esquire. Vargas will likewise to the extent that he is able so to do without interfering with the production of art work acceptable for use in the publications published directly or indirectly by Esquire endeavor to produce art work of a commercial nature of the character which shall from time to time be specified by Esquire with a view to Esquire's exploiting the commercial use of such art work, through such channels and with such means and for such uses as Esquire shall from time to time see fit. During the term of this employment agreement Vargas shall not produce any art work of any kind or character whatsoever for any other person, firm or corporation save and except Esquire and none of the art work produced by Vargas or resulting from his assistance or bearing his name shall be used, sold or in any manner exploited save and except by Esquire under the terms of this agreement.

3. As compensation for his services Esquire shall pay to Vargas while this agreement shall remain in effect the sum of Seventy-five Dollars ($75.00) per week, payable monthly. As additional compensation Esquire shall pay to Vargas fifty per centum (50%) of the net receipts of Esquire from the sale or other disposition of art work produced by Vargas which is sold or exploited by Esquire for commercial purposes as distinguished from the art work which is utilized by Esquire or any of its subsidiary or affiliated companies for their own publications and ventures.

4. Esquire shall have the option of extending the term of this agreement from and after July 1, 1943 for an additional period of three years upon giving to Vargas not less than ninety (90) days prior to July 1, 1943 written notice of its election so to do. In the event of such extension Vargas' basic salary during such extended period shall be One Hundred Fifty Dollars ($150.00) per week and he shall receive sixty per centum (60%) of the net receipts above described.

5. This agreement shall not be cancellable by Vargas for any reason whatsoever and it is mutually agreed and understood that the services to be rendered by Vargas are unique in character and cannot be duplicated and that Esquire shall be entitled in case of the failure, neglect or refusal of Vargas to carry out, observe and perform all of the covenants, duties and obligations assumed by him

hereunder to obtain relief by way of either prohibitory or mandatory injunctions or both or to obtain any other relief either at law or in equity which will assure to Esquire the full benefit during the term of this agreement of the services which Vargas has herein undertaken to render and perform.

6. Esquire shall be permitted to cancel this agreement in the event that the art material furnished by Vargas fails to meet the reasonable standards set by Esquire or it is determined by the editor of Esquire that Vargas is failing to produce in reasonable quantities art work of such acceptable character as to be usable in the publications published by Esquire or its subsidiary or affiliated companies, or in the event of Vargas' failure to faithfully carry out and discharge the duties and obligations of the employment arrangement set forth in this agreement.

In Witness Whereof the parties hereto have caused this agreement to be duly executed this 20th day of June, 1940.

Esquire, Inc.,
By David A. Smart,
President,

Attest:

_____

Secretary.

Alberto Vargas. (Seal)

Immediately after signing the contract, Alberto rushed to catch the 20th Century Limited. On the train ride back to New York to collect his belongings and wind up his affairs, Alberto wrote Anna the following: "The Editor also remarked that I had been master of the air brush long before the world heard of Petty. . . . In other words as an artist I am *already* made, as a money-making proposition they will make me, that in a few words is the substance and essence of the whole thing. . . . I have never seen a more enthusiastic bunch of people about my work!"

He returned to Chicago and, taking an efficiency apartment on Walton Street near *Esquire* offices, set to work with Smart to produce the first painting, scheduled for the October issue.

Smart had seen a number of thirty-by-forty sanguine chalk sketches in Alberto's portfolio that he particularly liked, and one of these was chosen to be finished for the magazine. This was a horizontal pose, and much turmoil ensued in adapting it to the vertical position, which Smart felt was imperative. At Smart's direction Alberto clothed the nude figure in a sheer bathing suit and added a telephone as an overt dig at Petty.

Meanwhile, by airmail, Anna Mae tried to calm her ego-ecstatic husband. The couple had gone from despair to ten-foot-tall euphoria in a matter of a few days. In her

The final barely clothed version appeared amidst much promotional hubbub in the October 1940 issue of *Esquire.*

Anna Mae, sun-
dappled and pensive,
sits with the kids—
Poocho and
Jitters—in Chicago's
Lincoln Park.

letter of July 2, she cautioned him against letting the publisher know that he had any plans to eventually return to California. She assured him that she and the "kids" would be with him soon.

Shortly before she left for Chicago, Anna Mae received another exultant letter from her lonely husband: "It is the *first time* since the good old days of Shadowland that a fellow has recognized my talent and has let me go ahead and be myself for a change . . . As an artist I am *reborn* . . . My motto these days: my heart belongs to my wife, my soul to my maker; but my art belongs to Esquire!!!" A few years hence the latter statement would prove to be grotesquely accurate and understated.

When Anna Mae arrived in Chicago, Alberto began to settle down. Her very presence was a tranquilizer. Shortly after her arrival, Smart called them to his office, explained that the girl feature would be called by the artist's name, and asked if it would be agreeable to them if they dropped the *s* in Vargas; he found the "Varga Girl" more euphonious than the "Vargas Girl." Neither of the Vargases was in the mood or position to argue over such an apparently insignificant point. (Socially, in fact in every way but legally, Vargas became "Varga.")

The engraver was quickly called and, at the last minute, the *s* on the signature of the completed October engravings was killed.

"Varga" was born.

Thereafter, only 14 out of a total of 180 individual paintings that appeared in *Esquire* carried a hand signature. Instead, a type slug signature developed at Smart's direction was used. Rarely after 1941 did the artist sign his paintings. It wasn't necessary. All of his freelance work, however, was hand signed.

Where Smart had a few weeks earlier felt totally frustrated by the Petty deal, he now knew that he had a wedge. If he could immediately get the name "Varga" before the public, and if they went for it, he would be able to stop being humble—a position totally intolerable to his nature—and get rid of George Petty as soon as the 1941 contract expired.

He quickly set the magazine's entire promotion department into action. House ads, mailers, window cards—every possible means of spreading "Varga's" name was pressed into service.

Smart knew that he needed one big blast to get the nation's attention, and he thought he had it when he remembered a Petty Girl premium calendar that Old Gold had offered for 1940. Within a few weeks of the contract's signing, he invited the Vargases to his home to discuss something important. He proposed a calendar consisting of twelve paintings that would run in the December issue and be offered to the readers through the mail. He felt that it would, if successful, ensure Alberto's quick acceptance by the public.

Initially six paintings were to be in color, six in black and white. After seeing Alberto's rushed sketches he decided for total color. The first "Varga" Calendar appeared after only two "Varga" paintings had appeared in *Esquire*. Its success was instantaneous: through mail order only, it sold 320,000 copies at twenty-five cents each. By 1946 the figure would be just short of 3,000,000.

The New Yorker's "Talk of the Town" column in the January 11, 1941, issue commented:

> Uncertain of the future, but fearing the worst, we read a prospectus about the 1941 calendar that *Esquire* is urging on its readers—a dozen pages of nepenthe, each illustrated by Varga, an artist who could make a girl look nude if she were rolled up in a rug. "Order it, look at it, feel it quiver; set it to the music of a slow drum," said the announcement. "The Varga Calendar, festooned with girls faultless in limb and shaping, girls curved with strange magics, girls of eggshell smoothness and the warmth of monsoons, has been printed in the full, lush colors of life—to bring you pulsing dreams throughout each siesta and vigil of the passing year . . . its heartening message, spelled with the turn of a thigh or the lift of a hip." This may be just the thing we need right now. A little concentration and perhaps we can visualize each month as a separate and lovely encounter with a beautiful stranger, the whole year a harmless and joyous trip through the old seraglio. It is nice to think of *Esquire* readers joyfully awaiting the turning of each page, identifying each four weeks with a new delight. Skipping ahead, we are now in a position to tell you what is in store for you. August, the invasion month, is a cutie lying prone on a beach, covered slightly by a transparent hat. October, when the sky may be full of bombers, is a slip of a girl bared from toe to hip, shooting an arrow. November, when the mists may be rolling over the Channel, perhaps as a shroud, will be a blonde in a dress as tight and as white as the skin over the knuckles of your fist. What may be the end of the world will be marked by a nice thigh, the beginning of chaos by the lift of a pretty hip. That's the year ahead of you, gentlemen. Feel it quiver. Set it to the music of a slow drum.

Smart was stunned and delighted by such free publicity. He knew he had his Girl. Petty, somewhat put out, demanded that he be given the calendar assignment. Smart made it clear that any future calendars would be done by Varga.

Gingrich, conversely, had done what he could, and would have done more, to keep Petty at *Esquire*. He had

Seen here in a 1942 photo, teenage model Jeanne Dean would have an indelible effect on the form of the "Varga(s)" Girl.

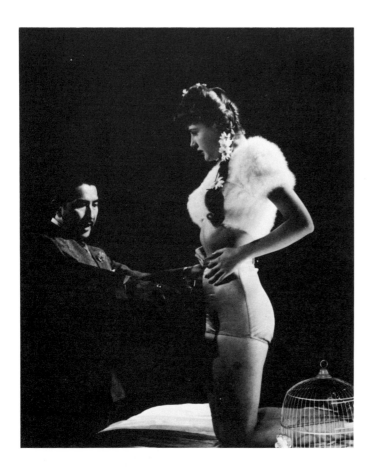

Alberto in 1942 on the set of M-G-M's *DuBarry Was a Lady,* posing Kay Aldrich *(above)* and Georgia Carroll for the film's "Varga" Calendar sequence. Great beauties, both girls were Conover models whose features would blend into many a future "Varga" Girl.

always liked the Petty Girl, considering the "Varga" Girl "meretricious."*

Included in Smart's frantic promotional efforts: an extraordinary uni-buttocked variation of the first calendar's August page, which quickly became "Jan," Jantzen's widely promoted image for their new Suntan oil; a stiff-as-a-board-awful, full-length portrait of Deitrich for Universal's *Flame of New Orleans*; a sample painting quickly loaned to West Point's *Pointer* magazine for their spring 1941 issue. Smart knew exactly which side of the bread his war was buttered on. His savvy was awesome and urgent.

For the Vargases 1941 was a dizzily glorious year. Alberto's talent, Smart's connections, and the *Esquire* name garnered major advertisers such as MGM, Jantzen, 20th Century Fox, Universal Studios, Acme Beer, Sealy Mattress Co., and Raymond Laboratories.

Fox received one of Alberto's best pieces—a languid full-length portrait of Betty Grable in a bathing suit—for *Moon Over Miami.* It is perhaps the ultimate pinup. The "Varga" Playing Cards, which were introduced that summer, became an instant success. One of the pair of paintings used for this deck carries a unique distinction: a nude with no nipples.

Alberto had initially used Anna Mae as his model, but Smart peremptorily objected so a petite fifteen-year-old beauty with glorious titian hair, Jeanne Dean, became his primary model throughout 1941 and 1942. She was shy, snowcovered, and came chaperoned the day she met the Vargases. After that first meeting, Jeanne's mother never played guardian again. Jeanne would have a profound effect on the Vargas Girl throughout Alberto's career. She went to Hollywood in 1943 for a fling at starletdom, and when the Vargases returned to Westwood in 1946 she again posed for Alberto. Today a still stunning, wind-blown, freckle-faced woman, living in Malibu with three children, five horses, two dogs, and a cat, she recalls the Vargases' closeness, "like one person," and remembers that she was allowed no publicity as the "Varga" Girl model: "I gather that a real girl would have destroyed the fantasy that men built around Mr. Vargas'

---

*Gingrich, incidentally, would exhibit one of publishing's most remarkable memory lapses in his publisher's page, in *Esquire*'s October 1971 issue, "Welcome Back to the Forties." When writing of the enormous wartime popularity of the magazine's gatefold pinups, he would attribute them generally and specifically—the post office suit and the five-page foldout of January 1946—to George Petty. All very fascinating and dreadfully misleading. Petty did not produce a single editorial painting for anyone from December 1941 until January 1945, when his work appeared regularly in *True* magazine.

paintings."*

Well before the debacle of Pearl Harbor, *Esquire* began cruising full steam ahead into militarism and unabashed patriotism, with the "Varga" Girl as its proudly promoted figurehead. Her popularity soared as the war grew louder.

Alberto's advertising work in 1942 included a major promotion for MGM's *DuBarry Was a Lady*, in which the "Varga" Calendar came to rhythmic, undulating life. Upon his arrival at Metro to help promote the film, Alberto reveled in the red carpet treatment he received from the very people who had put him down two years earlier. In addition to this and his broadening duties for the magazine, he began to do sketches and paintings requested as "mascots" by various units of the armed forces. Every request was fulfilled.

Throughout 1943, 1944, and most of 1945 his days were devoted to finishing paintings, his nights to developing new sketches and special drawings for the Armed Forces—nights when Frances Langford's recording of "I'm in the Mood for Love" might repeat and repeat; nights that often stretched into bleary-eyed, bird-filled Lake Michigan dawns.

Typical of these requests was the following from Chaplain C. A. Sullivan of the Seabees:

> Nothing other than a 30-day leave in the States would satisfy the Seabees scattered throughout the Pacific as much as a Varga Girl dedicated and drawn for them. Since the majority of our personnel are serving on isolated islands, we entertain them through a regimental newspaper, the Seabeecon. . . . Would it be at all possible for you to send us a Varga Girl for publication in our paper?

The "Varga" Girl had become the repository of thousands of servicemen's dreams, and a synonym for the newly popular phrase "pinup girl." Interestingly, a large proportion of Alberto's paintings lacked the thing *most* indigenous to pinups: direct eye contact. Many of the girls gazed into space dreamily or looked away from the reader at someone or something else.†

By 1945 the annual gross sale of all "Varga" byproducts would be well over the million mark. Vargas'

*Sociological Note: The first two paintings showed nipple covered only by sheer fabric, and a bit of nudity was sprinkled throughout the first calendar, which was of course painted at that same time. Thereafter, very little nudity was admitted. The war years were remarkably puritanical—even breast and buttock cleavage were minimized.

† An interesting fact is that about 25 percent of the artist's fan mail was and is from women wishing to emulate the image projected.

The original drawing (top) selected by M-G-M for their *Dubarry* ad campaign. They opted to avoid censorial ire by having a lace ruffle added to the bra top and another ruffle added to the apron (bottom). This succeeded, unfortunately, in ruining the entire flow of the figure.

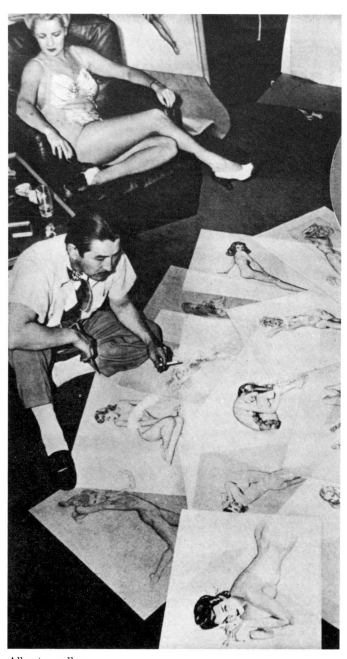

Alberto, vellum sketches, and Charlotte Gold shown in the Vargas apartment. Charlotte never posed for Alberto—she just happened to be handy for this photo session.

days and nights became a virtual marathon of work. To-day, when recalling the 1940s, the artist registers bewilderment at his energy. Like pain, the precise memory is spared, but you know it happened.

It is necessary to give the reader some understanding of the Vargases' unusual relationship with their publisher. Early in their association they began referring to him as "Uncle David" and often Smart referred to Alberto as "Young Man"—though the two men were approximately the same age. Smart quietly directed their lives, encouraging and helping them to select a distinctive apartment at 936 Lake Shore Drive and appropriate furnishings for it. But when the couple showed interest in a home in the suburbs, he discouraged them, preferring that they remain near the *Esquire* offices in the Palmolive Building.

From the beginning of their association, being aware of just how far seventy-five dollars per week would go in light of the life-style he insisted upon for them, Smart had told the Vargases that if they needed any funds, they had simply to ask, and he would have the accounting department issue a check. Although it was not explained to them, this was in effect a system of advances against earnings. No statements were ever issued the Vargases while Alberto was employed by *Esquire.* The thankful couple had a childlike admiration for and trust in "Uncle David," and were therefore somewhat condescendingly treated as children. Smart found it a most effective way to get what he wanted.†

In August of 1943 the "Varga" Girl's national prominence was assured when the United States Postal Department issued *Esquire* a summons, on grounds of obscenity, to show cause why it should continue to enjoy fourth-class mailing privileges; Alberto's Girl was named as the prime offender. No one is really sure why it all happened, but with the final decision in *Esquire*'s favor, it was certain that, although the lengthy court case had been costly to the magazine, it had reaped a bumper crop of publicity, using the "Varga" Girl to obtain most of it. (Alberto had even done a special drawing of a Girl in hoopskirt and bonnet as the possible costume for future "Varga" Girls, should the Post Office win.)

The Vargases had been married for thirteen years. Childless, they were utterly devoted to and totally de-

*By December of 1944, with no effort at all, they were in hock to the dandy tune of $5,395.40.
†At one point in 1941, when Smart was in some *very* serious legal difficulties, Alberto told Anna Mae that he would work for the man for nothing if necessary. The couple's gratitude and affection for "Uncle David" were boundless. They felt they owed him everything.

pendent on one another. They went out seldom, entertained even less. Loners, with purpose and reason—they lived for Alberto's art. His work, his health, his happiness were first and foremost to Anna Mae Vargas.

Vargas' contract was up for renewal in July 1943. Using his inability to give employees increases under the wartime Wage Stabilization Act as his excuse, Smart delayed drawing up a new contract until the early part of 1944, when it was decided that wages could be increased by making Alberto an independent contractor rather than a staff artist. To quote Smart from the trial transcript:

> Well . . . I have given considerable thought to this existing contract that will run out very shortly . . . and although you know that we have an option which would extend this contract for another three years, by increasing your salary double, and giving you a slight increase in outside promotion work (advertising) I am of the feeling that, notwithstanding the fact that we are in a war period now and notwithstanding the fact that it is a pretty good increase, and notwithstanding the fact that at this time there is a Wage Stabilization Act, we are not going to take advantage of that option, although we could. . . . I have confirmed the fact with our counsel that, this contract having been signed before the Wage Stabilization Act was in effect . . . we could continue this contract by the mere fact of writing you a letter, so stating.
>
> I have in mind a new contract. I think you have made progress. I think you have honestly given every bit of effort you are capable of, to do the things that this magazine has asked you to do. In view of that we would like to show our appreciation of that effort by giving you a new contract which would substantially be better than the one that we can right now make.

In the summer of 1943, Smart allowed Alberto to negotiate his own contract with Hearst's *American Weekly* for a series of twelve paintings aimed at specific branches of the armed forces, for which he received fifteen hundred dollars a painting. This and the Andrew Jergens Company's "Be His Pin-Up" ad campaign were the major outside work done in 1943.

That fall, when Alberto was deeply involved in the *American Weekly* series,* which ran into the winter of 1944, Smart told him that he wanted a new and different "Varga" Girl for the back covers of the military edition of the magazine, which was sold at cost to the armed forces and carried no advertising.

He explained that it was a bonus for the G.I.'s and Alberto readily complied. Though this may have

*It must be noted that the *American Weekly* was *weekly*. Each painting had a newspaper deadline.

Two examples of the extensive Jergens campaign of 1943. This series would have extended into 1944, but David Smart blew his top when he found out that Jergens ad agency had talked Alberto into signing an exclusive contract. Smart knew *everyone*, so heads rolled and the contract was swiftly broken.

MILITARY SECRETS

Now, no one can peek
At this Book of the Week—
Its contents I HAVE to be coy;
Would certainly bar any
If he knew I dated a .....;
That boy in the Navy
Whose hair is so wavy
Would woo at right me at the roots
If he found that I
had a Leatherneck Guy
Who woos in romantic cahoots!

PAINTING BY VARGA
VERSE BY PHIL STACK

This gatefold coin-
cided with the U.S.
Post Office suit
against *Esquire* in
1943. Her costume, if
not her pose, was
more than usually
revealing, making
her ideal newspaper
fodder. She was
spread cross-country
giving newspapers a
little sex and the
magazine lots of pub-
licity.

bothered him, it never occurred to him to complain of any work added to his schedule—not to Anna Mae and certainly not to Smart. There were nineteen "Varga" Girls delivered for the military edition from December 1943 to May 1945, nine of which were tight vellum sketches.

These additional paintings helped to bring Alberto's total output for *Esquire* alone in the calendar year of 1944 to a staggering forty-nine paintings. He literally had no idea of how much work he was doing. The engraver's delivery dates listed below will give some idea of his pell-mell pace:

1-6-44	1 (issue)	5-10-44	1 (calendar)
1-15-44	2 (cards)	5-15-44	2 (military)
1-20-44	2 (military edition)	5-22-44	1 (issue)
2-7-44	1 (issue)	5-26-44	1 (issue)
2-28-44	1 (issue)	6-13-44	1 (issue)
3-17-44	2 (military edition)	7-25-44	2 (military)
3-21-44	2 (calendar)	8-22-44	1 (issue)
3-24-44	1 (calendar)	9-6-44	2 (military)
3-29-44	1 (calendar)	10-17-44	1 (issue)
4-3-44	1 (issue)	11-15-44	2 (military)
4-11-44	2 (calendar)	11-16-44	5 (calendar)
4-18-44	2 (calendar)	11-21-44	1 (issue)
4-19-44	1 (calendar)	11-21-44	1 (calendar)
4-26-44	1 (calendar)	12-11-44	2 (calendar)
5-1-44	1 (calendar)	12-11-44	1 (issue)
5-6-44	1 (issue)	12-28-44	3 (calendar)

In spite of all this rush, pressure, and push, the quality of Alberto's work remained high. His command of frisket* produced a facility born of demand. This slickness became apparent by 1943. There were a few real lemons in the Vargas-*Esquire* crop and some boners. There were at least two six-fingered girls and one apparently one-armed girl. All in all, though, the average of hits was remarkably high. Another fascinating fact is that many paintings finished in the late 1940s and early 1950s were actually begun during this hectic time.

Toward the end of January 1944, a crack appeared in the solid wall of affection that the Vargases had felt for David Smart. A trip to Kansas and Nebraska seems a mundane enough premise for the first sign of strain on the seemingly ideal relationship.

A number of six-foot-tall blow-ups of "Varga" Girls were produced and hand-colored by Alberto for hanging in briefing stations in Wichita and Grand Island. Since *Esquire* had partially financed these buildings, the Army invited Smart and others he would choose to fly there in a B-25 for elaborate dedication ceremonies. Alberto was to go, of course, and Smart personally invited Anna Mae; then later he privately told Alberto that the group going

*A translucent paper used as a stencil in airbrushing.

to Kansas would be "stag."

At a luncheon for those going to Kansas held the day before the flight, at which Anna Mae was present, Smart was asked by someone at the table exactly who was going. The small list included a New York model and Smart's wife. Being quite open and direct, Anna Mae asked, "And why am I not going, Mr. Smart?" The answer was reportedly an equally direct "Because there's no room." He then asked Anna Mae if she would entertain the group at her apartment for the afternoon, which she graciously did.

The trip lasted four days—four miserable days for Anna Mae and particularly for Alberto. Asked constantly who his inspiration was, he kept dragging out his wallet and showing his dear wife's picture. Displaying his chagrin in the only way he knew, he flew both ways perched in the Plexiglas nose cone of the all-but-empty B-25 plane, and during meals ate with the delighted enlisted men to avoid the company at the VIP table. After an evening meal at the Grand Island Station with combat crew 102-34, Alberto created a minor furor while autographing 1944 "Varga" calendars: he insisted that the men autograph a calendar for him—"After all, they were doing the fighting."

At the VIP table, there was controlled consternation when "Uncle David" became aware of the attention his artistic lamb was being accorded—in truth, for the first time in almost twenty years Alberto felt the power of himself as a man and an artist, if only briefly.

Returning to Chicago, Smart soon knew that he had a problem. When he called to ask if anything was wrong, Anna Mae told him in emotional and spirited words how she felt at being deliberately separated from her husband in this rare moment of recognition. Bitter words flew between the two. Smart asked the Vargases to come to his office the following day, when he accused the couple of turning on him, which was unconscionable. As he so aptly put it in his later trial testimony, "'Mrs. Vargas, it pains me to have you take on this way. . . . If you feel what you say as strongly as you do, it seems to me, in view of the fact that there is no contract existent between us, wouldn't this be a good time for you to go your way, and let the magazine go its way?' As I recall it, that had a rather sobering effect on Mrs. Vargas."

Both artist and wife offered deep apologies for Anna Mae's actions, at which Smart expansively suggested that they forget the whole thing. Thereafter things returned to an apparent norm.

Coincidental with this incident, Michael Todd, the Bantam Barnum of Broadway, commissioned Alberto, with Smart's eager approval, to do a composite painting

Miss December 1944 smiles contentedly wreathed in the enthusiastic signatures of Combat Crew 102–134.

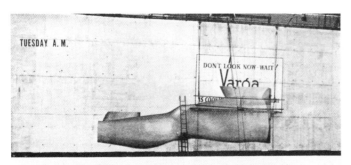

BROADWAY VARGA GIRL

Advertising "Mexican Hayride,"

she goes up in sections on sign

The Broadway musical comedy *Mexican Hayride* is long on legs. To advertise it, Producer Mike Todd commissioned Alberto Varga to draw a Varga girl for the huge sign over the Winter Garden Theatre where his show is currently playing. The girl was to be a composite picture of his star, June Havoc, and all the other lovelies in the show. On April 7th, to the gaping astonishment of thousands of Broadwayites who jammed the sidewalks and stalled traffic to watch, the sign was finished. It was terrific. The legs alone,

with shoes, of the bewitching miss were 71 feet long. Varga first made a sketch. Then workmen painted 31 sections onto weatherproofed Flexboard. The sign was put up like a jigsaw puzzle, each section fitting into the one next to it. A LIFE photographer recorded the 10-day process of construction, the pictures here being labeled with the day each was taken. First things—the legs (*see above and below*)—came first. The ankle and the foot were one piece. The knee-cap was another. For what happened later, turn the page.

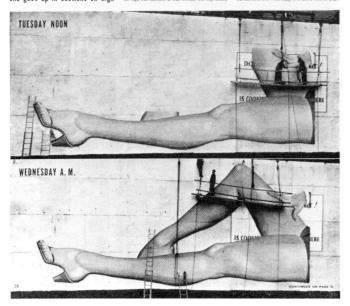

CONTINUED ON PAGE 41

The publicity genius of Michael Todd reached new heights with the installation of this block-long "Varga" Girl above New York's Winter Garden Theatre, advertising his musical *Mexican Hayride*. The photo coverage of this happening filled newspapers nationwide, and such diverse magazines as *Life* and *Mechanix Illustrated*.

for his new musical production, *Mexican Hayride.* In a massive publicity campaign Todd had the painting enlarged in thirty-one sections and installed on the block-long billboard above the Winter Garden Theatre. It took ten days to install (a process breathlessly recorded by *Life* magazine) and instantly became a national sensation. Thousands thronged Broadway speculating on her vital statistics. Her legs alone were a colossal seventy feet long. It was Alberto's only advertising work in 1944. There is no known record of his having received payment for this work.

Meanwhile, *Esquire*'s legal counsel had drafted the long-delayed new contract from a memorandum drawn up by Smart's brother, Alfred, on May 10, 1944. Much later, John Bartizal, *Esquire*'s comptroller and assistant treasurer, would testify to the following incident. After Bartizal had examined the finished contract, he talked to Alfred and together they went to see Smart in his office. "I gave Mr. David Smart the same information I had given Alfred Smart, called his attention to the fact that the earnings for '44 under the [new] contract probably would not equal the earnings for '43 [because there had been considerably less outside work] and he said that he appreciated that, but that *he could always give him more if he wanted to* [author's italics], more than required in the contract." This conversation was never disputed by *Esquire*'s counsel.

The new contract was ready for signing. The scene was set. Smart invited the Vargases to his office for the signing on May 23, 1944. Before they arrived he called his brother, Alfred, and Bartizal, asking them to stand by and await his call—they would be needed as witnesses to the contract.

The Vargases arrived at 2:30 and were greeted warmly by Smart. The air was filled with an effusion of mutual admiration. When they were seated at his desk, Smart quickly read a few brief portions of the contract and suggested that Alberto go over to his conference table and look the contract over. He talked to Anna Mae for a moment and then called his brother and Bartizal. Alberto sat down, counted the number of pages in the contract, and then began looking at it. Alfred Smart and Bartizal entered the room. Greetings were exchanged and Alberto rose from his seat and joined the happy group around Smart's desk. Smart asked if he was ready to sign. Alberto said yes. At this point in his testimony, Smart says: "I did say, 'Alberto,' and I addressed myself to Mr. Vargas and his wife, 'this represents a distinct improvement from the story of where you came in on your first contract. I think it is most equitable. I think it is one that will earn you considerable money, and I think it should be an incentive to do your very best.'"

It took less than thirty minutes, from entrance to exit, to complete the entire transaction. After the elated couple left, Bartizal asked if after notarizing the contract he should send a copy to the Vargases. He was told to file it and give them one when they asked for it.

For the Vargases this was a long-imagined dream come true. Security and full recognition for Alberto! They were ecstatic.

Anna Mae did not ask for a copy of the contract until June 1945, and only then because the first raise in the eighteen-month escalation clause had come due and it had to be explained to her by Bartizal. It did not even occur to her then to ask for a copy. She had to be asked if she wanted it.

For the reader to assess the importance of this matter, it is necessary to reproduce the 1944 contract in toto. It is a difficult matter for it touches on aspects of mutual obligation and trust. The document was, and is today, remarkable. That the Vargases signed it is perhaps even more remarkable.

1944 Contract

Agreement made as of January 1, 1944, between Esquire, Inc., hereinafter called "Esquire," and Alberto Vargas, hereinafter called "Vargas,"

Witnesseth.

For approximately the past three years Vargas has been preparing and furnishing to Esquire drawings for use by Esquire in connection with its publications and other printed merchandise;

In connection with certain of these drawings, the name "Varga," "Varga Girl," and similar names have been given national publicity by Esquire and have become well known to the public. Vargas acknowledges that the success of the drawings has been due primarily to the guidance which Esquire has given him and to the publicity given to them by Esquire's publications;

The parties now desire to enter into an agreement defining their mutual rights and obligations.

Accordingly, the parties hereto agree as follows:

1. Vargas agrees for a period of ten years and six months, beginning January 1, 1944, as an independent contractor, to supply Esquire with not less than twenty-six (26) drawings during each six-month period. Vargas will endeavor to make said drawings satisfactory to Esquire and of a quality and standard comparable to the drawings which have heretofore been furnished by Vargas to Esquire. The drawings so furnished, and also the name "Varga," "Varga Girl," "Varga, Esq.," and any and all other names, designs or material used in connection therewith, shall forever belong exclusively to Esquire,

After the Jeep was changed, this sketch for the *Journal American* would salute the Army's Tank Corps.

This grimly real War Department photo of the marine landing at Tarawa caught an incongruously lighthearted stowaway—a very carefully folded and refolded "Varga" Girl—a tribute to her portability and to what she symbolized to the American fighting man.

and Esquire shall have all rights with respect thereto, including (without limiting the generality of the foregoing) the right to use, lease, sell or otherwise dispose of the same as it shall see fit, and all radio, motion picture and reprint rights. Esquire shall also have the right to copyright any of said drawings, names, designs or material or take any other action it shall deem advisable for the purpose of protecting its rights therein.

2. In consideration of the drawings so furnished and of the other rights herein given to Esquire, Esquire shall pay to Vargas the following amounts, namely: Eighteen Thousand ($18,000.00) Dollars during the first eighteen-months' period beginning January 1, 1944, and during each succeeding eighteen-months' period of the term of this agreement, an amount equal to the amount paid during the next preceding eighteen-months' period, increased by Fifteen Hundred ($1,500.00) Dollars. Payments of these amounts shall be made to Vargas in equal monthly installments during each eighteen-month period.

In addition, Esquire shall pay to Vargas one-fourth (1/4) of one percent (1%) of gross receipts actually received by Esquire from the commercial sale of articles, booklets, reprints, calendars, etc. (exclusive of magazines and similar publications) sold by Esquire during the term of this agreement, containing reproductions of any drawings furnished to Esquire by Vargas under this agreement. Payment of any amounts based upon gross receipts shall be made semi-annually within three (3) months after the end of each semi-annual period. Any articles given away or distributed by Esquire for promotional purposes shall not be deemed to be sold within the meaning of this paragraph.

3. During the term of this agreement Vargas will not create for or furnish to anyone other than Esquire any drawings of any kind or character; and for a period of three (3) years after the expiration or cancelation of this agreement, he will not furnish any drawings created by him to be used by him or anyone else as a part of or in connection with the manufacture or distribution of any products, which are in competition with any of the products manufactured, produced, sold, or distributed by Esquire.

4. It is understood that Esquire shall have the right to cancel this agreement at the end of the second or any succeeding eighteen-months' period of the term of this agreement, upon giving to Vargas not less than six months' notice in writing of such cancelation; and, in the event of such cancelation, neither party shall after the effective date of cancelation have any obligation hereunder to the other party, except on account of rights accrued prior to such effective date, and except as otherwise herein expressly provided. The words "term of this Agreement" as used in this agreement shall be deemed to mean the period from January 1, 1944, to July 1, 1954, or, if this agreement be canceled prior thereto, then to the

effective date of such cancelation.

5. Any notice required or permitted to be given hereunder shall be deemed to be sufficiently given if sent by registered mail, postage prepaid, addressed, if to Esquire, at 919 North Michigan Avenue, Chicago 11, Illinois.

6. This agreement shall inure to the benefit of and shall be enforceable by Esquire, its successors and assigns.

In Witness Whereof, Vargas has hereunto set his hand and seal, and Esquire has caused this instrument to be executed by its officer thereunto duly organized this 23rd day of May, 1944.

Alberto Vargas,   (Seal)

Witness:
Anna Mae Vargas.

Esquire, Inc.,
*By David A. Smart,
President.*

(Seal)
Attest:
*Alfred Smart,
Secretary*
Witness:
John R. Bartizal.

The "Varga" Calendar for 1947 carried no credit for the artist. It carried instead the heading The Esquire Girl Calendar.

Eventually, one supposes, the Vargases would have examined the document, but the issue would soon be forced upon them.

In November 1944, the quintessential "Varga" Girl appeared.*She combined the utmost abstract surrealism with popular appeal. An impossible physical image was unquestioningly accepted by a supposedly naïve age. (In the sixties, it would be necessary to indicate some support for the girl's body.)

Alberto's naturalization as an American citizen in early 1945 got lost in a blur of work, work, and more work. In June of 1945 at a meeting with Smart, Alberto expressed his desire to take a vacation. He was exhausted. Smart convinced him to delay his trip until the fall, when it would be cooler. He also wanted to be certain that Alberto was well ahead with his work and, as a special favor, he particularly wanted the 1947 calendar finished before he left. He explained that because of the war ending, paper shortages, possible strikes, new competition, and vast editorial changes in the magazine, *Esquire* had to keep one step ahead of the rest. Alberto acquiesced.

August 1945. Peace and joy filled the land. It was all but unnoticed at 936 Lake Shore Drive in the frenzy of fluttering tissue sketches that built the 1947 calendar.

Smart had other, more immediate problems in 1945. He was chronically subject to violent migraine headaches which could hold him inoperative for days at a time. He

*(See page 95.)

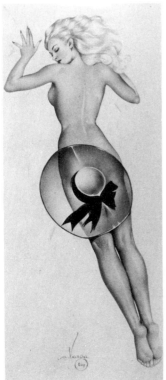

The rushed painting of a nude Jan *(left)* for Jantzen's Tanning Oil somehow became well suited by the time she appeared in print. Beyond a fascination with big hats and this pose, the 1948 "Varga" Calendar page *(opposite page)* illustrates the artist's increasing interest in capturing bone, muscle, fat and flesh, moving away from the simplicity and stylization of the Art Deco thirties and forties.

had tried all imaginable cures, including a Chinese acupuncturist in Paris in 1937. All to no avail.

Furthermore, Arnold Gingrich took the war's end as an opportunity to retire to Switzerland. By the 1940s he had had it. Smart more and more dictated editorial policy. According to Gingrich, Smart's personality was somewhat "abrasive," though "butter wouldn't melt in his mouth when he wanted something." By then, in his words, "Dave had become the Universal Genius." Sops to the war effort and Gingrich's acute sense of the magazine's wartime editorial effeteness reinforced his decision to "retire."

The "new competition" came primarily from Fawcett Publications' *True* magazine, which in January of 1945 took on a totally new personality. From a hairy-chested, field-and-stream type of operation, *True* suddenly blossomed out with something of the character and freshness of the early *Esquire*, without all the fashions and sophistication, without Fitzgerald and Hemingway, but with the Petty Girl at her hefty, hearty, hybrid best, which must indeed have irked Smart.

Alberto had just delivered the November 1945 gatefold finish, and returned three days later with sixteen vellum sketches, some of which he had worked on the previous winter "just for emergencies." Smart picked twelve for the calendar and two for the gatefold. Alberto expressed his concern that his styling might look out-of-date because of his having worked so far in advance on the paintings. Smart waved that away.

By this time Alberto had virtually ceased using a model. He used photos, Anna Mae, and particularly his imagination. His mind was so filled with poses and images that he could, with the aid of the dozens of sketches he had made in the past, work from memory.

Working sixteen to eighteen hours a day, as he had throughout 1944, he finished the entire calendar and the December, January, February, and March gatefolds in nine weeks. The January 1946 painting was to be a special holiday multiple-gatefold opening out to a length of three and one-half feet. It had to be rendered most meticulously since it would be reproduced same-size.

Returning at the end of October from their usual vacation, a cross-country motor trip, Alberto, feeling more tired than rested, went immediately to Smart's office. Smart welcomed him back and told him it was imperative that he plan on producing a painting a week, getting on an assembly line until he got far in advance on his work. This was uncharacteristic of Smart's usual method of getting work out of Alberto.

Soon Alberto called Smart and said that he had a large

group of sketches ready for the upcoming year's gatefolds—could he come over and have a look?

Smart entered with little or no greeting. The Vargases
immediately sensed something odd. The publisher circled
the spread-out sketches silently. In Alberto's words, "It
was as though someone had cholera." When he ventured
the opinion that these were his best things, Smart re-
torted that they stank, that if these were the best, there
would be no more "Varga" Girl, and abruptly walked out.

Then Smart called to say that he had to have sketches
for April and May immediately. Within a day two
sketches were okayed, and when Alberto delivered the
finished one for April, he was told to get to work on the
1946–47 playing cards because they were needed immediately. Smart didn't like any of the initial sketches
and became irritable and more than usually contentious,
voicing his displeasure in no uncertain terms.

Finally, in the middle of December, two sketches were
okayed. When Alberto delivered the finished paintings
and the final vellum sketch of a bride for the June issue,
Smart seemed pleased. As Alberto gathered his things to
leave, the publisher redundantly referred to getting on
the production line.

Nonplussed, wits and nerves frayed, Alberto finally
broke and pleaded for a reason for all this rushing—he
was six months ahead in his work. Smart answered force-
fully that he simply must get busy and produce *one a
week*. When Alberto expressed bewilderment, Smart
tersely stated that it was in the contract and suggested
he go home and read it.

It was Anna Mae, reading the document for the first
time, who understood one thing with terrible clarity:
"not less than twenty-six (26) drawings during each six
months' period." That caused instant shock. Struggling
with the wording of the compensation clause created
doubt and confusion. The remainder of the contract went
unread. The hapless couple sat alone, very frightened.

They didn't know what to do. A concerned and sym-
pathetic employee of *Esquire*, after spelling out the details of the contract, urged them, in confidence, to seek
legal counsel. The Christmas holiday was a dreamlike
mix of the normal and abnormal. Alberto delivered the
May finished art. Perfunctory words were spoken between publisher and artist. Anna Mae sent the usually
hand-delivered gifts to the Smarts' house. Smart came to
their apartment to wish them a Merry Christmas and
thank them for the gifts. The contract was never mentioned. Smart sent the following telegram on December
31, 1945: "Just to tell you that 1945 is a good year to have
behind us and now with the war over, *Esquire* and Al-

Smart allowed an annual painting for Acme Beer apparently to reach the common man—the non-*Esquire* reader. This calmly athletic woman from 1946 is clearly inspired by Georgia Carroll and clearly and successfully defies all known laws of gravity.

berto will have a fresh future to do greater things. Mrs. Smart joins me in wishing you both a Happy New Year." Thinking the situation could be settled without resorting to lawyers, the Vargases made an appointment with Smart on January 9.

Confronting him with their hurt and humiliation, the usually reticent Alberto expressed himself in anguish: "Twenty-six pictures every six months, minimum, means that you are requiring one every week for ten years; if you want one a day, that word 'minimum' means exactly that. That, Mr. Smart, is a physical impossibility that I couldn't do for my own father if I was a machine. They have to come from the heart, through my hand. I could not live two years." Smart said that he had never intended to hold him to that.

When they began discussing salary, Smart lost control of his temper and any order to the discussion dissolved into an ugly, incoherent melee. Smart, thrown off guard, with controlled fury finally ordered them to go home and cool off, saying he would reread the contract and call them in a few days.

Four days later, the second meeting began more calmly, but upon the subject of the number of paintings and money, it was again reduced to a smoldering, ugly shambles, ending with Smart's threat to see to it that Alberto never made another drawing for anyone in the United States. Leaving, Anna Mae replied, "In that case, Mr. Smart, all we have is our courage and each other. We have no fear when we have that."

Within hours Smart ordered the engraver to kill the "Varga" Girl and signature slugs on the April gatefold. The last two paintings and the 1947 calendar ran with a new designation: "The Esquire Girl."

In the District Court on Tuesday, April 30, 1946, more than four years of bitter litigation began. The first round, case number 9209, *Alberto Vargas*, Plaintiff v. *Esquire, Inc.*, Defendant, Judge Michael L. Igoe presiding, ended on May 20, 1946, the court finding in favor of Alberto Vargas, Plaintiff.

On May 4, 1946, a patent was requested on all typeform and signature slug uses pertaining to the "Varga" Girl. Patent #436,779 was issued to *Esquire*, Incorporated on February 17, 1948.

Esquire appealed the lower court's finding on August 16, 1946. The Circuit Court of Appeals reversed the decision on February 27, 1948. The dissenting judge in that decision offered the following opinion:

> . . . His (Vargas') knowledge of business, such as finance and contracts, must have been meager in the beginning and was not enhanced during all the time he did

business with Smart. The situation did not suggest, much less require, that he pay any attention to such matters. He was an artist and his time and energy were confined to that field. It is doubtful if he had any inclination and certainly no reason to do otherwise, because he had often been assured by Smart that he need not worry or concern himself with financial matters but that they would be taken care of by Smart. It is quite plain that Smart desired plaintiff to devote himself in toto to the production of art. It perhaps is true, as asserted by the defendant (Esquire), that it was good business on the part of Smart to accord to plaintiff the generous treatment which the record discloses. Such altruistic treatment, however, did not dispel, in fact it succored, the trust and confidence engendered in the plaintiff.

The majority having refused to accept the finding of the District Court that a special relationship of trust and confidence existed between plaintiff and the defendant, there is no occasion to go farther. Evidently this is the vital and controlling issue in the case and the only purpose of this dissent is to enter my protest to what, in my judgment, is a usurpation by this court of a function so clearly lodged in the District Court.

Appeals and counterappeals followed, the brouhaha resulting eventually in *Esquire*'s countersuit.

The second case, numbers 10216 and 10217, *Esquire Inc.*, Plaintiff-Appellee v. *Varga Enterprises, Inc.* and *Alberto Vargas*, Defendants-Appellants, Judge William J. Campbell presiding, began in February 1948 and ended June 8, 1950, the court finding in favor of *Esquire Inc.*, Plaintiff.

"Varga" was dead.

What were Smart's motives? On one occasion in mid-December he told Alberto and *Esquire*'s production manager of his plan to run two "Varga" Girls each month. Both men demurred and the subject was dropped. Within three weeks, at the first of the heated contract discussions, he announced that he was thinking of running the "Varga" Girl every *other* month—confused and contradictory statements.

Facts: The 1944 contract bound the artist utterly and exclusively until 1957. Thereafter the name "Varga" could not be used by the artist. The artist and his "Varga" Girl were becoming ever more famous and valuable properties. The notoriety attendant on the coincidental postal suit and Todd billboard had made the "Varga" Girl a national institution.

Conjecture: With the war and its restrictions out of the way, with deeper editorial involvement on his part, with new and vital competition and circulation worries, Smart found it frustrating to have to pussyfoot around a personal relationship that hindered him from getting what

UNITED STATES PATENT OFFICE

Esquire, Inc., Chicago, Ill.

Act of March 19, 1920

Application May 4, 1946, Serial No. 501,446

THE VARGA GIRL

STATEMENT

Esquire, Inc., a corporation duly organized under the laws of the State of Delaware and located at Chicago, Illinois, and doing business at 919 North Michigan Avenue, Chicago, Illinois, has adopted and used the trade-mark shown in the accompanying drawing, for a SECTION OR FEATURE IN A PERIODICAL PUBLICATION, in Class 38, Prints and publications, and presents herewith five specimens showing the trade-mark as actually used by applicant upon the goods, and requests that the same be registered in the United States Patent Office in accordance with the act of March 19, 1920.

The trade-mark has been continuously used and applied to said goods in applicant's business since January of 1943, and has been in bona fide use for not less than one year in interstate commerce by the applicant.

The trade-mark is applied or affixed to the goods by printing, embossing, or in some other manner applying the trade-mark directly thereto.

ESQUIRE, INC.,
By ALFRED SMART,
Secretary & Treasurer.

The Vargas suit against *Esquire* began on April 30, 1946. *Esquire* requested a patent on all type form uses of the name "Varga" on May 4, 1946.

"Varga" Enterprises published its own calendar for 1948. By February of that year *Esquire* had distribution halted on grounds of copyright infringement and use of their patented material.

he wanted, what the contract called for: fifty-two paintings by Vargas every year. Since the Kansas trip snub of Anna Mae, the couple's attitude toward Smart had cooled ever so slightly. Most certainly aware of this, the publisher no doubt felt that if the puppy-dog devotion of the artist was lost, then a strong, binding contract would be necessary to keep a tight grip on the situation. Once the contract was signed, and there was little reason to think it wouldn't be, Smart would have Alberto right where he wanted him. He wanted the relationship on a strictly business basis. He had a headache.

The whole affair was so thoroughly personal, based on unique and diverse personalities and their successful interaction, that it is impossible to imagine that David Smart seriously believed any other tactic would produce the desired result. He wanted the "Varga" Girl but didn't want Vargas, wanted the creation, not the creator. He had a terrible headache.

Guesswork aside, Smart can be accused of handling the final moments of the marriage ingloriously, whatever his motivation. The contract speaks for itself. It is willful, if not malicious, in its intent to protect *Esquire* (Smart) at any and all cost. He undoubtedly felt that the "Varga" Girl was his and should forever be his. Anyway, artists went out of fashion—they didn't go on painting forever.

Early in 1951 Alfred Smart suddenly and unexpectedly died. Two years David's junior, a health nut, he never smoked or took pills and in every way lived a moderate life diametrically opposed to David's.

Alfred's impossible passing terrorized David. During a late-night phone call from Smart concerning Alfred's death, Gingrich felt that "it was immediately apparent that if he (Smart) couldn't let out some of the pressure that was building up . . . he would as a thinking entity almost entirely disintegrate."

Gingrich relates that though he had shared a number of dark personal crises, he had never known a death to affect anyone as shatteringly as Alfred's did David—for the obvious reason that he had never known anyone capable of such emotional extremes.

Within a year of Alfred's demise Smart's physician, during a routine inspection, discovered a minute intestinal polyp. The doctors insisted that the polyp was innocuous, requiring little more than periodic checks, but Smart, ever the hypochondriac and perfectionist, was repulsed by the thought of something in him that didn't belong there and demanded it be removed.

The operation was essentially a simple one, but because Smart had taken so much medication, both remedial and preventative, for so many years, his body was unable to respond properly to the necessary postoperative medication and he died shortly afterward (in 1952), at the age of sixty.

The perfunctory trial data given previously hide a complex mixture of joy and misery. After the first trial the couple moved back to their bungalow in Los Angeles and became embroiled in all sorts of get-rich-quick schemes. The very nature of Alberto's art and the trial itself attracted genuinely interested businessmen as well as circus types, con artists, and assorted quacks. The latter questionable associations resulted in some pretty pulpy press-agentry, such as the phrase "Vargalure," as in "Ann Corio has 'Vargalure.'"

Offers for everything from nudie decalcomania glasses to a Howard Hughes-produced "Varga" Girl film flooded the couple. In mid-1946 "Varga" Enterprises was formed but after issuing its 1948 "Varga" calendar, both the corporation and the printer were enjoined from further enterprise by *Esquire*.

Fawcett Publications commissioned an extended series of portraits of stars for their *Motion Picture* magazine in 1947 while the second trial was in preparation. Before the first painting hit the newsstands, *Esquire* let it be known that the outcome of the decision regarding the Vargas contract wasn't settled and that even though the court had decided in the artist's favor, *Esquire* was appealing that decision.

Fawcett killed the series after only four paintings had appeared: studies of Linda Darnell, Ann Sheridan, Hedy Lamarr, and Ava Gardner. Paramount Pictures also managed to slip one in: a full-length portrait of Paulette Goddard for a 1946 production, *Suddenly It's Spring*.

The 1950 decision in *Esquire*'s favor brought it all to a halt. There was no "Varga" Girl. There was no "Varga." It was as though six years of the Vargases' lives had never been.

With the court decision came the irrevocable realization for Alberto that he would have to begin again. Paintings would have to be signed *Vargas*. It was the worst of times: the explanations, the negative shaking of heads, the lowering of prices . . .

The desperate couple treaded water in an ocean of debt. Trial costs were astronomical for an artist who literally had nothing to show for more than five years as *Esquire*'s star performer and major breadwinner—less than nothing, since Alberto left the magazine owing it $4,259.25! Well, they did have a $728 fur coat, a $2,250 diamond ring, a $5,000 trip to America for Alberto's mother and sister, some furniture and fame in name—a name now taken away.

The artist and his Junoesque Miss Universe, circa 1948. This publicity stunt garnered considerable attention in that Alberto used Linda Darnell's face, Jeanne Dean's bust and waist, and Marie Windsor's hips and limbs. This painting can be seen on page 106.

Alice Ann Kelley,
Miss Junior America
1948, was the last to
have a portrait
painted bearing the
signature "Varga."

Alberto's lawyer had optimistically assumed that the case would be won and his fee settled easily. Since this was not the case and since, in fact, he had involved himself corporately with the doomed "Varga" Enterprises, his only recourse was to take 10 percent of any and all of Alberto's subsequent earnings. It would be 1975 before this debt was satisfied.

In 1950 Anna Mae had a radical mastectomy for which their doctor loaned the money.

Finally, their bungalow was under a triple mortgage.

Alberto tried everything to make money, even product design: scarves, neckties, toiletries, and lingerie. At great cost, sets of transparencies of his latest work were sent to various magazines and agencies. But little came of this effort.

What did materialize barely supported the couple and their creditors: royalties on playing cards published by the Creative Playing Card Company; a three-year (1954–57) series published monthly in the British pocket-sized magazine *Men Only*; a few posters for a brewery; a superb portrait of Shelley Winters used by RKO to advertise their 1952 film *Behave Yourself*; and an eight-month series of starlet discoveries done in 1951 for *True* magazine.

Meanwhile, in 1953, with more brass than gold, a young man in Chicago named Hugh Hefner began publishing a haphazard magazine called *Playboy*. By 1956 a great many people were becoming aware of the increasing success of this unpretentious upstart. Friends brought the Vargases' attention to the magazine's potential. Never had nudity been so vividly used in a nationally circulated magazine, and Anna Mae became convinced that here was the only hope for publication of Alberto's work, particularly the never-published large nudes which he had been working on since the early 1940s.

Taking another loan on the mortgage on their bungalow to finance the trip, the couple headed for Chicago and *Playboy*. Hefner was very impressed by Alberto's large nudes, feeling, indeed, that they were far and away the best work Alberto had ever done. He told them, however, that he didn't feel he could commit himself to any regular use of Vargas. The time didn't seem right to him and, quite frankly, *Playboy* could not afford it.

He did propose doing a pictorial spread on the nudes, and the Vargases readily agreed. Though not what they had hoped for, the money from this was badly needed. It would have to do.

They left *Playboy*'s offices with Hefner's promise that he would see when, how, and if he could work Vargas into the magazine.

The couple returned to Los Angeles, waiting, hoping to hear something from *Playboy*. When a year passed and all hope had faded, fate in the form of the Peruvian government directed their next move.

The government of Peru invited their Arequipanian brother to bring his work to Lima for a major exhibit and offered to pay half the expenses of the trip. Alberto was overjoyed. This was something he had dreamed of for years, and here it was being offered on a platter. He and his bride would see his homeland together.

In August of 1958, dozens of his paintings covering every period of Vargas' work were carefully crated and loaded onto the freighter that took the excited couple to Lima. Their two-month stay in Lima and then Arequipa was unreal—filled with endless dinners and luncheons. Reporters hounded them. Newspapers and magazines devoted entire issues to his life and work. The then-President, at a luncheon in their honor, conferred upon Alberto the Medal and Brevit of Knighthood in the Order of the Sun. (That and a Citation for Meritorious Service, given him by the U.S. Treasury Department in 1945, are Alberto's proudest possessions.) Although his exhibitions in both cities attracted enthusiastic mobs, of greatest satisfaction to the artist was the presence of his aged father, whom he had not seen since 1911.

Upon Alberto's arrival in his hometown, the Arequipanians went wild over their native son, but the Vargases found peaceful escape in the spaciousness and beauty of their surroundings. When asked if Arequipa had changed much since he had seen it as a child, Alberto's answer was a resounding, "Thank the Lord, no!"

Returning to the realities of life in the United States, the Vargases found nothing changed. The following eighteen months were grim and workless; their heavily mortgaged house was in imminent danger of foreclosure. Alberto was ready and willing to work, but there were no takers. The art community thought him dead, if they thought of him at all.

I became associate art director of *Playboy* in June of 1959. Having been a long-time Vargas admirer, and aware of *Playboy*'s 1957 Vargas nudes pictorial, I periodically suggested using Vargas in the magazine.

I kept this up with embarrassing regularity, to no avail. Finally I dug up some negatives of Vargas paintings not used in the 1957 feature, blew them up to poster proportions, and pinned them up where they couldn't be missed by anyone passing my office door.

One great day Hefner went by my office on his way to see Art Paul, *Playboy*'s art director; he passed, and suddenly returning, stuck his head in my doorway, looked at

Another "Varga" Enterprises product that got little further than this counter card because of the loss of name to *Esquire*.

"Legacy Nude #1": Begun in 1939, this languorous, stunningly legged blonde wouldn't be finished until 1949. Many of Alberto's finest private works were begun in the frantic forties and finished in the lean fifties.

The potential of this sketch *(left)* prompted plans to run the model's face on a *Playboy* cover. When the finish arrived, apparent stage fright had caused the face to alter, causing some consternation. Another go-round in the artist's studio produced the editorially perfect ingenue features promised by

the sketch and she graced the March 1965 cover *(opposite page)*. Fashion note: Though difficult to fathom today, it would have been editorially incomprehensible to have the sheer fabric of her gown cross her bust—thus the breast-feeding aspect of its design— nothing should interrupt the view.

the Vargas photostats, not at me, and said one word: "Maybe."

Within a few months, despite heavy editorial opposition, Hefner introduced the Vargas Girl into *Playboy* on a wait-and-see basis. I was delighted. More important, and unknown to me at the time, the Vargases were tearfully grateful to whatever forces ruled their lives. Their gratitude to Hefner has never ended.

The 1950s, though cash-as-catch-can commercially, were aesthetically superb.

The large (up to thirty-by-forty) busman's holiday watercolors begun in the 1940s were brought to full and brilliant realization, his technique pushed to its apparent limits. Twelve of these were set aside as a legacy for Anna Mae, not to be sold in his lifetime. A number of them are published here for the first time.

By the 1950s, Alberto unconsciously began to divide his commercial work from his private work. This was most apparent in his early months with *Playboy*. The first two paintings were pickups—meticulous nudes from his own stock. The third painting, which is best forgotten, bridged the artistic gap. The next, which appeared in December 1960, was the first done from scratch specifically for the magazine

It exhibited a light, youthful freshness new to his work and an obviously lighter, looser, technique, which would grow generally looser throughout his astonishing tenure with *Playboy*. Meanwhile, work on his large private stock virtually ceased, with his total absorption in *Playboy* work, and wasn't reactivated until 1975.

Hefner's personal interest in the Vargas Girl was as proprietary as David Smart's had been in the "Varga" Girl, but pronounced character differences effected a harmony that brought to the Vargases a peace never even dreamed of.

I began acting Lucky Pierre to Hefner and Vargas sometime in 1961.

Memories of nit-picking, cigarette-dry, pill- and Pepsi-spiked wee-hour meetings debating the annual clutch of twelve tissue sketches for the upcoming issues attest to Hefner's abiding concern about the Vargas Girl.

I admit to constantly expecting too much of the artist and self-consciously committing some rather quirky art direction in the name of progressive company man.

Hef's blind spot was his total inability to kill a tissue (and a love of "beehive" hairdos). No matter how lost the cause, he would thrive on it for hours, struggling to save the single stinker because he fancied her hairdo, face, right buttock, or God knows what. He invariably won the battle over an up-since-6:30 editor, and the final painting was invariably a bummer.

During and because of his tenure at *Playboy*, Alberto received and refused many bids for his services, not only from American firms, but from organizations in England, Germany, and Italy as well. All were avoided in his singular desire to please "El Hefe."

Apropos of Alberto's previously mentioned tromp l'oeil quality, Hefner once objected to the fact that in a particular painting the girl's left eye was lower than her right eye. When this detail was dutifully brought to the artist's attention, he expressed bewilderment: "Who ever saw anyone with even eyes? That's what makes the drawings real!"

Interesting Occurrences: Beginning with the fourth painting in *Playboy*, the average age of the Vargas Girl dropped from twenty-five to nineteen.

Because much searching couldn't unearth a black girl deemed suitable for the magazine's glossy Playmate foldout, Vargas was handed the task of creating the first nude Negro to grace *Playboy*'s feverishly liberal pages.

Because certain superstars would not strip for the magazine's celebrity-hungry photographers, Alberto once again played surrogate with six sub-rosa simulacrums of the screen's finest. Originally planned as a multipaged takeout, the likenesses were altered at the last minute when Hefner got nervous about publishing the likes of Liz Taylor in the nude.

Oddly, the only thing that has given Alberto any real trouble during his lengthy residence at *Playboy* has been the magazine's discovery of pubic hair. He had a problem adapting to the "new freedom." To quote the artist: "It was something that was simply never done in my commercial work. I was a little bashful about it at the beginning because of Anna Mae. . . . She wondered if it was really necessary." Many would share her doubts.

Alberto has enjoyed his longest, most fruitful association with Hugh Hefner. No contract, just an agreement between two gentlemen. Due to this association, the mortgages that had hung over the Vargases' heads for years were paid in full in 1965.

This mutual regard and respect is well illustrated by a letter of February 8, 1968, from Arthur Paul regarding a rare visit to Chicago:

> As you know, the Vargases were here spreading sunlight. . . . I've come to the conclusion that Alberto is a man who knows how to love. Some of his charm and stamina come from his ancestry, but his skill as an artist was an early endeavor that blossomed as he did. May he live forever.

The warmth between artist, wife, and publisher shows

In 1968 during a rare trip the Vargases were invited to stay at the now defunct Chicago Playboy Mansion. The highlight was an evening spent with El Hefe.

in the following exchange. From a telegram dated June 9, 1966, and sent to Mr. and Mrs. Alberto Vargas at the Playboy Club in Los Angeles:

> Congratulations on this your 36th wedding anniversary, marking another year of marital bliss for you, another year of your creativity for us. May both these happy unions continue for many years to come.
>
> Love,
> Hef

On June 12, 1966, Anna Mae replied:

> Dear Hef:
> On June 9th I sat proudly next to my precious husband on our 36th anniversary—at the Playboy Club—where we felt the spirit of "our Hef" guiding us through the most exquisite evening of our lives.
> The dinner was superb—champagne so delicious. The flower arrangement—with white orchid corsage—was most beautiful. Most of all your warm telegram arrived to make our evening complete.
> What a wonderful person you are—so sensitive and compassionate. We are so fortunate to know you, and as a friend. Too bad there are not many more people like you. It would make our world a better place in which to live. I believe love conquers All.
> I wish I could give you a big hug—and thank you in person for what you do for us. This comes from deep in my heart.
>
> Love and affection,
> Anna Mae

Because of its proximity to us in time, the value of the *Playboy* work (152 paintings over a sixteen-year period) is difficult to stamp. In the main it seems to reflect the times. The 1960s were in general troublesome, as is some of what we've seen of the 1970s. Most self-centered artistic expression is suppressed in order to accommodate insistent editorial demand for "variety." Only through nostalgia can we find glamour and mystery. If that sounds grumpy, so be it.

At its best it shows brilliance and a fairly consistent command of technique that with more freedom might have produced many stronger, more straightforward, less gimmicky paintings. Dispassionate judgment will have to wait for another generation.

On November 7, 1974, Alberto Vargas was faced with the most incomprehensible and brutal ordeal of his life— the death of his "Beloved Ana," a woman frail in old age, of awesome strength, who combined compassion with candor, and whose overwhelming concern was protecting her husband and nurturing his talent. They learned from each other as they loved each other. Their relationship was as one—unusually close by any standard; and if any-thing can be said to have sustained Alberto through the terrible reality of her death it is the reality of their love.

To define Joaquin Alberto Vargas, his purpose and goals, we quote again from the initial 1946 *"Varga"-Esquire* trial transcript. The questioner is the lawyer for the defendant, *Esquire*:

> **Q.** Now, do you recall your testimony of the other day . . . in which you said, "I told him time and time again that I will someday make a Varga Girl so beautiful, so perfect, so typical of the American girl, that I can put that picture in any part of the world, without any signa-ture . . . and they will say, that is the Varga Girl."
> **A.** Yes, sir.
> **Q.** When did you reach that point?
> **A.** I haven't reached it yet.
> **Q.** You haven't reached it yet?
> **A.** No, sir.

I think we can safely assume for Alberto Vargas that he has reached that point.

Mr. and Mrs. Alberto Vargas on their thirty-sixth wedding anniversary at the Los Angeles Playboy Club—June 9, 1966.

Much of the artist's
work from the twen-
ties has been lost.
This charming study
was found in a garage
in 1972.

Anna Mae Clift,
1920, 13″ x 18″.

Anna Mae Clift,
1920, approx. 26″ x
38″.

"Kimono Girl #2,"
posed by Kathlyn
Martyn.

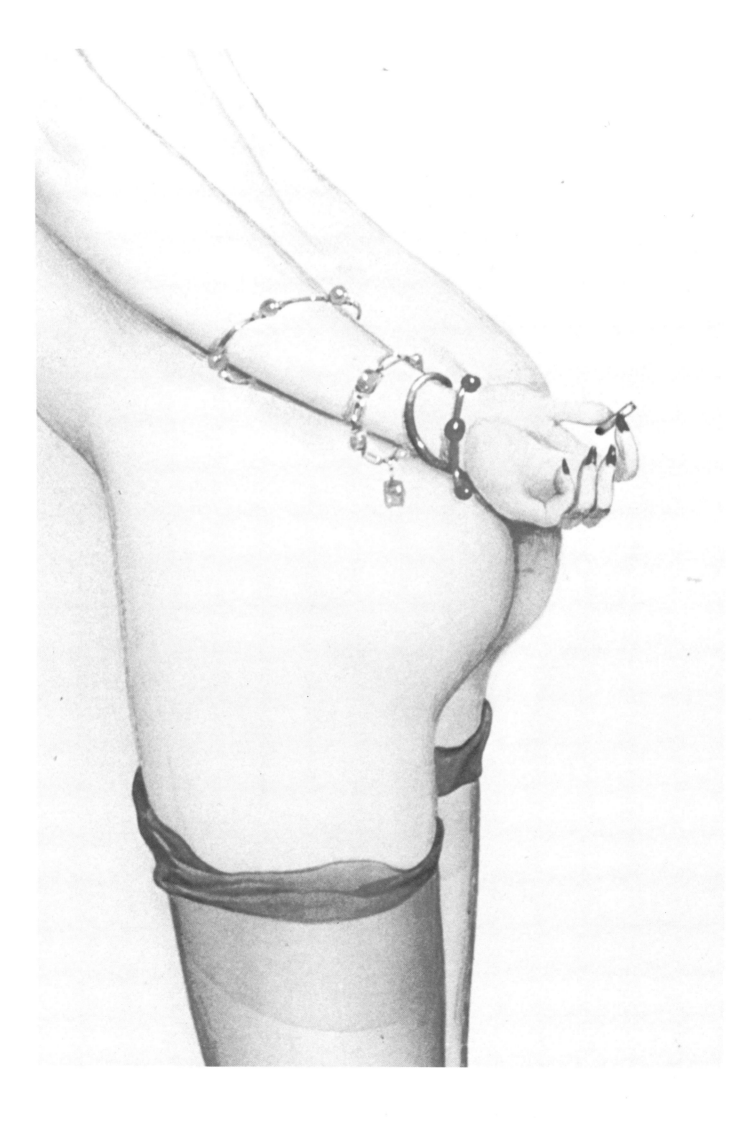

The 20's and the Follies

"Red Stockings," 1921
approx. 24″ x 38″.

Top left: Portrait
posed by Cornelia
Rogers 1927.

Top right: "Beige
Blonde," circa 1925.

Bottom left: "Grape
Girl," 1918.

Bottom right: "Peru-
vian Girl," circa 1920.

With the success of
his *Ziegfeld Follies*
poster work, which
began in 1919, inter-
est in the young
Peruvian artist in-
creased. Among the
earliest commissions
is this eloquently agi-
tated Art Nouveau
portrait of Norma
Talmadge for the
February 1920 issue
of *Theatre Magazine*.

Theatre Magazine

TITLE REG.-U.S.PAT.OFF.

ALBERT
VARGAS
M.C.M.XX

SS NORMA TALMADGE

FEBRUARY, 1920
VOL.XXXI NO.228
35 Cents $4.00 a Y

"Behind the Scenes,"
posed by Miami for
*Shadowland
Magazine*, 1922.

"Butterflies," posed
by Anna Mae Clift,
*Shadowland
Magazine*, 1922.

A severely damaged
Ziegfeld poster, circa
1920, was reclaimed
in part when the art-
ist managed to pre-
serve this beautifully
composed lower por-
tion. Approx. 17″ x
20″.

"A Live Wire," Zieg-
feld poster, *Shadow-
land Magazine*,
1921.

"YOUR HEALTH"

"Smoke Dreams,"
1927, 22″ x 26″.

"Lederle Plaque,"
circa 1920.

"Memory of Olive
Thomas," 1920, ap-
prox. 18″ x 24″.

"Beauty and the
Beast," 1925, ap-
prox. 20″ x 30″.

"Scheherazade,"
posed by Marie Pre-
vost, 1928, approx.
18″ x 24″.

Helen McCarthy,
1926, approx. 12″ x
16″.

Nita Naldi, 1923, approx. 26″ x 24″.

"Fleurs du Mal,"
1920. Reproduction
rights were subse-
quently sold to Para-
mount for a Miriam
Hopkins epic called
"Song of Songs" in
1931.

The 30's and Hollywood

"Deco Venus," circa 1930,
approx. 12″ x 18″.

Two examples of
French-inspired
fashion plates with
which the artist
hoped to open new
avenues of income,
circa 1931. *Right:*
"Cloche du Matin,"
9″ x 9″. *Opposite
page:* "Robe du
Apres-Midi,"
16″ x 20″.

Top: Warner Baxter.
Bottom: John Bowles.

Opposite page:

Rochelle Hudson.
Alice Faye.

Anna Sten.
Claire Trevor.

Detail from program
cover for the Motion
Picture Association.
Annual Hollywood
Masque Ball, 1930.

Happy Alice Faye with her pastel portrait by Vargas who pasteled every major 20th Century-Fox star in 1934.

Caja Erick, 1930, 9″x
12″, watercolor.

"Garbo Image," pastel, 1935, 18″ x 24″.

"The Last Follies,"
pastel, 1931, 18″ x 24″.

Sultry Stanwyck
gets the Vargas
treatment in this
1933 poster.

Light and lively Shirley Temple in pastel, and loose watercolor sketch for the final oil portrait that became part of the Fox Commissary mural.

31 - 36

High 30
Widest 3 5m

O.K.
Gertrude Temple

"He Loves Me,"
1939, 18″ x 22″.

"Pink Balloon," 1938,
18″ x 22″.

"Grey and Red,"
posed by Anna Mae
Vargas, circa 1932.

Two studies involving a favorite prop, both of which evolved from drawings done in the twenties.

Top: "Martini Time," 1935, approx. 18″ x 22″.

Bottom: "Black Notes," 1936, 24″ x 36″.

"Intrusion," 1933, 18″
x 24″.

"Diana," circa 1930,
26″ x 38″. (This paint-
ing appeared in the
March 1941 issue of
Esquire with the girl
attired in a long
green gown, which
had been painted on
an overlay.)

"The Green Room,"
circa 1935, 18″ x 24″,
pastel unsigned.

"Imogene Wilson
Fantasy," circa 1930,
18″ x 24″, pastel un-
signed.

The 40's and the "Varga" Girl

Esquire magazine gatefold,
June 1943.

The portrait of Betty Grable through the combination of artist and model produced the ultimate pin-up image, 1941.

Vivian Blaine, as a newcomer to Hollywood, profited by being idealized in a heavily promoted "Varga" campaign, 1943.

Though the artist preferred working directly from models or his own photographs, his initial rushed work for *Esquire* sometimes produced fanciful imagery from mundane sources such as the cosmetic ad above right. *Below: Esquire* magazine gatefold, January 1940.

"Virtue Triumphs,"
Esquire magazine
gatefold, November
1943.

THE VARGA GIRL.

VIRTUE TRIUMPHS!

The look of alarm
On this bundle of charm
    May set up some foolish illusions.
Her state of attire
May also inspire
    Some rather ignoble conclusions.
Perhaps you've surmised
That the gal's been surprised
    By a villainous sort of a louse—
But, brother, you're wrong,
You've been wrong right along—
    It wasn't a wolf . . . but a mouse!

PAINTING BY VARGA
VERSE BY PHIL STACK

"Lament for a
Pin-Up Pip,"
November 1944.

The original sketch
for November 1944
gatefold.

THE VARGA GIRL

LAMENT FOR A PIN-UP PIP!

*We've pinned you up in barracks
And we've raved about your charms,
We've had you up in bombers
And we've had you under arms,
We've idolized you, Honey,
We've really made a fuss
And say, you've got an awful nerve
To turn your back on us!*

**PAINTING BY VARGA
VERSE BY PHIL STACK**

The original sketch
for April 1945
"Varga" Calendar.

The original sketch
for November 1945
"Varga" Calendar.

"Peace, It's Wonder-
ful!", *Esquire*
magazine gatefold,
April 1943.

"There'll Always Be a Christmas." Original sketch and final gatefold, *Esquire* magazine, December 1943.

There'll Always Be a Christmas

As we stir a Toddy this Heavenly Body
    Is winging her way through the sky,
Her pose is a sign that the going is fine
    And America's still flying high!
The pace has been hot and we've been through a lot
    And none of us look any younger,
But "Mussy" is sunk and Tojo feels punk
    And Hitler is strictly from hunger!

"Hail and Farewell."
Original sketch and
final gatefold, *Es-
quire* magazine,
July 1943.

HAIL AND FAREWELL!

They have small time to clasp their new-found wonder . . .
A few short days and he is on his way . . .
As in a dream the war guns throb and thunder
To wound the magic of their Wedding Day . . .
Yet as he goes he carries in his keeping
Faith that will flame against the darkest night,
Love that will glow when leaden skies are weeping . . .
Honor and Pride to gird him for the fight;
He will come back to all he is defending
When victory has brought the world release . . .
A girl's warm smile to light the long day's ending
And nights that hold the lovely hush of peace;
(A peace they helped to shape with toil and tears—
Their Wedding Gift to all the future years!)

PAINTING BY VARGA
VERSE BY PHIL STACK

"Patriotic Gal," *Es-
quire* magazine,
gatefold April 1944.

"Warning Signal,"
Esquire magazine,
gatefold June 1945.

"Military Secrets,"
Esquire magazine
gatefold, February
1944.

"Matrimony Pre-
ferred," *Esquire*
magazine gatefold,
June 1944.

Among the artist's
most valued posses-
sions is this 1944
"Varga" Calendar
signed by a squadron
of Air Force men he
shared dinner with in
1944.

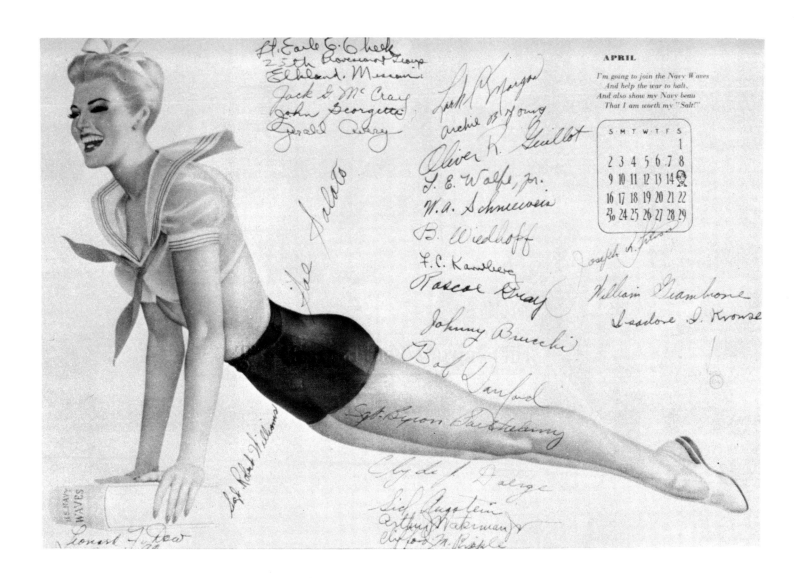

"Miss Universe,"
1948, 27″ x 36″.

"Ava Gardner,"
1947, approx. 24″ x
32″.

"Song for a Lost
Spring," *Esquire*
magazine gatefold,
May 1942.

Comprehensive
Jergens Powder Box
Design, 1943.

Sanguine chalk-
and-watercolor
sketch *(detail)* 1943.

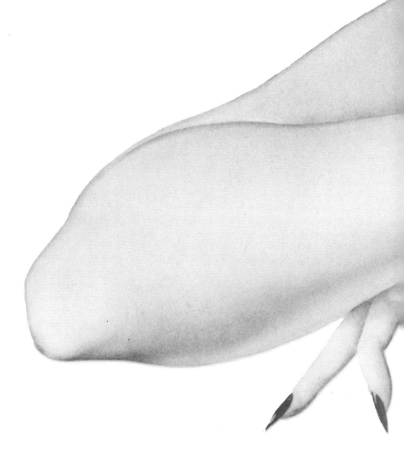

"Jane Russell," 1942.

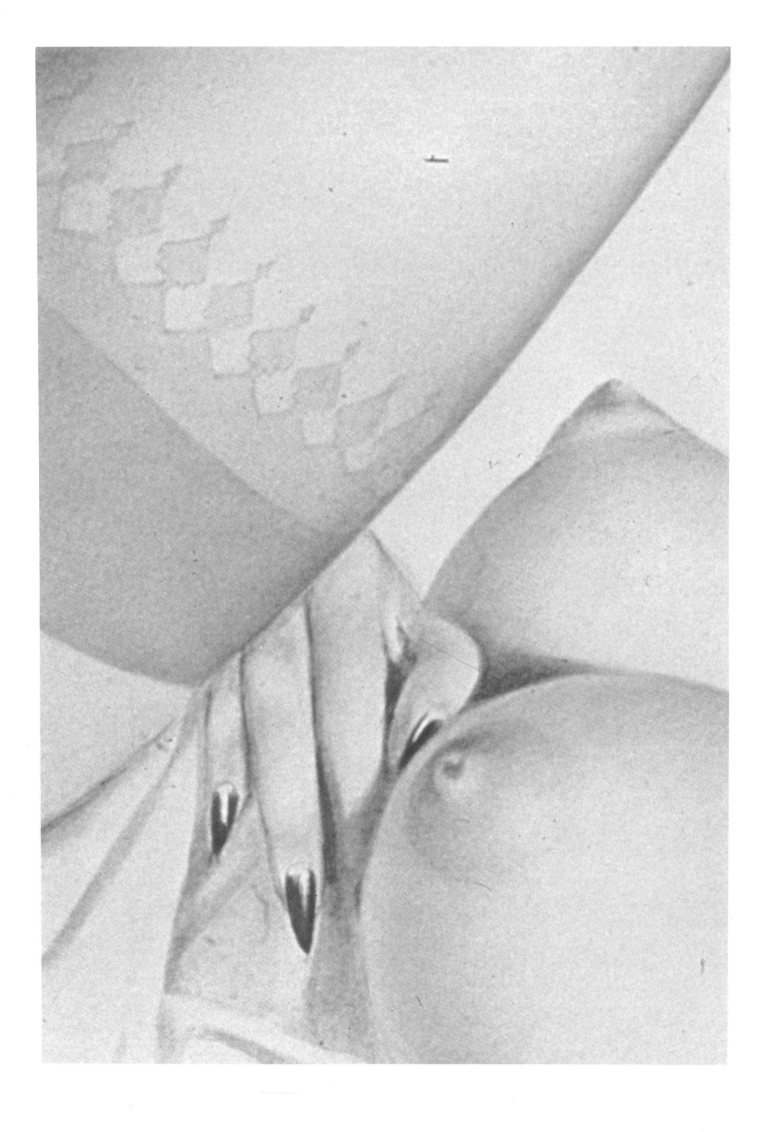

The 50's and the Vargas Girl

"Silk Stockings," circa 1956, approx. 26″ x 19″.

"Legacy Nude #8,"
1953, approx. 22″ x
36″.

"Marilyn Monroe,"
circa 1953, 15″ x 20″.

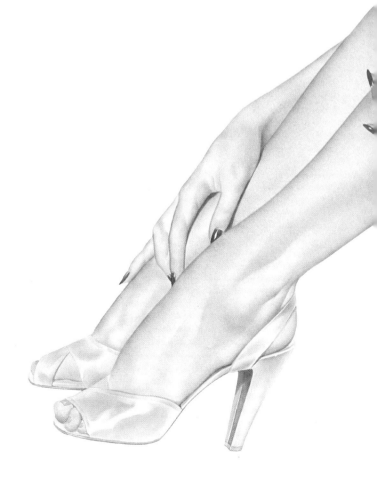

Legacy Nude #4,
"Cordillera de Los
Andes," 1950, posed
by Jeanne Dean.

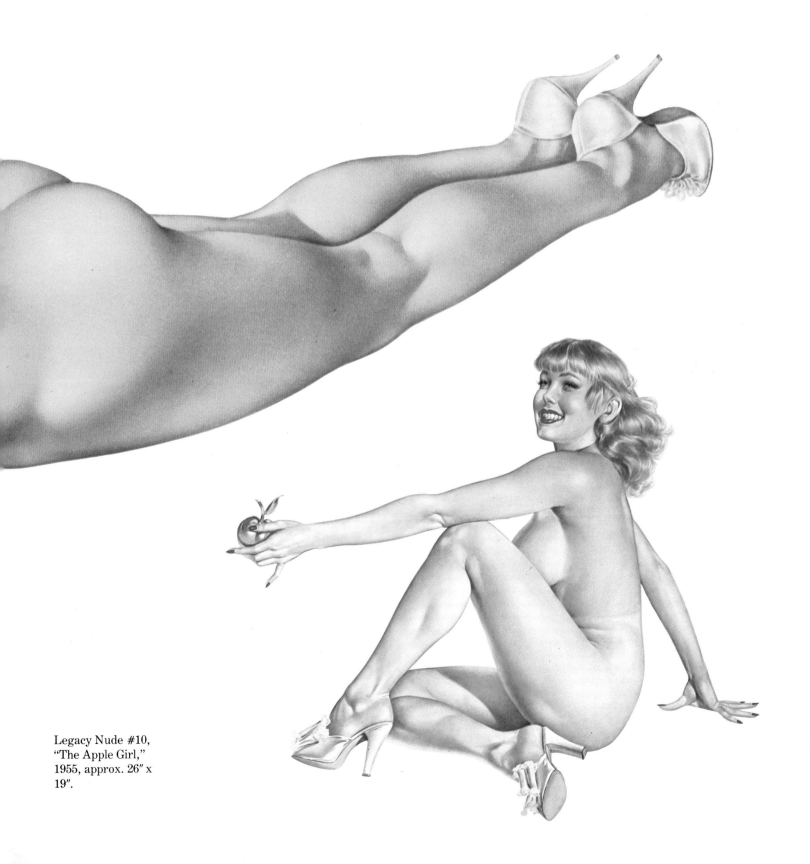

Legacy Nude #10,
"The Apple Girl,"
1955, approx. 26″ x
19″.

The 60's and the 70's

Playboy magazine,
March 1965.

Playboy magazine,
September, 1971.

Playboy magazine,
December 1963.

Playboy magazine,
January 1971.

Overleaf:
1975: When Jack O'Grady Communications began research for an ambitious series of bicentennial paintings slated to run in the *Chicago Tribune*, a number of Americans stationed abroad during World War II were asked what influences stood out in memories of those days. Two that popped up with impressive regularity were Glenn Miller's Air Force Band and the "Varga" Girl. As a result, Alberto was commissioned to paint his impression of the war. Regret and disillusionment are evident in this quietly tense and reflective work, which appeared in the Sunday, December 7, 1975, edition of the *Tribune*, an extraordinarily coincidental date. "World War II," 22" x 35".

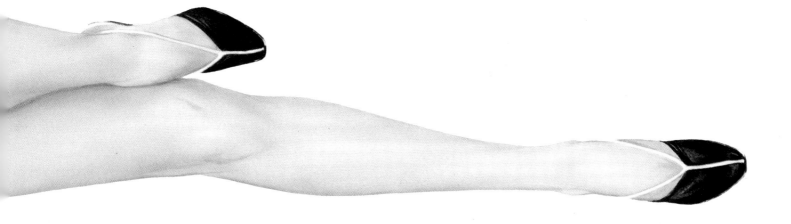

TECHNIQUE

First I do a series of very small, very quick rough sketches on cheap little pads I have. If one of these sketches strikes me, I concentrate on that one. I used to enlarge it by a square-graph method, but now I just begin to sketch it directly onto 24-by-36-inch tracing paper. This enlarged tissue sketch is refined as much as necessary, even if I have to do multiple tracings of the original. If I have serious doubts about anatomy, a model is called in at this point so I can verify whatever I've done. The model is also important for determining how light hits the body.

The final sketch is usually on heavy vellum which has a nice "tooth" for the chalks I use for such details as flesh tones. I use Conti Carre's sanguine chalk sticks for the basic flesh tone, adding a bit of brown for deeper shadows and for hair, and using blending stumps to spread the color. Heavy vellum will take some watercolor, so details like lips and eyes can be added in that medium. I end up with a very close approximation of the finished painting—very important if you are dealing with a publisher or ad agency, but, in most cases, I even do it for myself.

Transferring this final sketch to your watercolor board is the next step. I have two large pieces of medium-weight tracing paper, the backs of which have been coated, one with sanguine chalk, one with brown chalk. I have heavily coated these papers, hand rubbing the layers of chalk to a smooth finish. The excess chalk is of course shaken and brushed off as you're applying the layers. These are my master tracing sheets. Depending on the depth of flesh tone I'm planning, I choose one of the coated sheets and place it gently facedown on the final board. This is taped to the board to keep it from slipping. The vellum sketch is then placed over this and also taped in position.

Using a #9 pencil, I then go over my tissue. The outline I am now transferring to the board is quite faint.

When lifted off, any dust from the transfer sheet is removed with a soft sable dusting brush. Never make any hard erasures on your outline-board transfer! It will "bruise" the surface of the board and watercolor will gather in pockets or pools. Gently does it.

Now I wash my board. I take it outside my studio and hose it down with a fine spray. First the back, then the front. (This can be accomplished in your bathroom shower as well.) After letting the excess water run off one corner, I place it faceup on a waiting *clean* towel on my drawing board. Watch out for dust and dirt. It may have to be washed again if dust settles on the wet surface. Test the board for dryness by gently pressing the butt of your palm against the board. A portable heater will cut drying time to about an hour.

The surface may seem dry, but the entire board is damp, therefore "water-bearing."

If you could still buy Whatman Watercolor Board I would urge you to—it was the best. I have a series of direct sketches on Whatman just waiting to be done. I'm saving them for my old age. I can only tell you to buy the very best board available to you.

My flesh tint was arrived at over many years. I've used Windsor Newton selected-list tube colors since the 1920s, and their burnt sienna heavily diluted with water is my base flesh tint. It produces a polished ivory cast and contains all tints basic to flesh. I keep three 3-inch diameter white porcelain dishes with covers containing three graded sienna tones premixed before I begin to work. I add a touch of diluted brown for the darkest tint. You can add a touch of red, yellow—any tint in another dish producing special colorcasts to the flesh. The flesh is always my first concern since it is the single most important factor in my work.

Another important thing about those pots of watercolor tint. A doctor once advised me to put glycerine on a healing wound to keep it soft. I wondered what it would do to watercolor. It in no way affects the quality, and it does miraculously keep your water wet! It helps prevent evaporation, but do keep your tints tightly covered when not in use. More important, it gives tint a working flexibility.

To about ⅛ of a cup of ready-to-apply color add 3 or 4 drops of glycerine. This will almost give you the same effect as a damp board in aiding even color flow.

I again make certain the board is free of dust, grit, or dirt and then lay my first very pale tint over all exposed parts of the body—sometimes over everything, depending on costume and hair color.

After laying my basic pale ·sienna tint I wait a minute or two until the shine of the damp surface disappears. I then lay in a wash of tint about twice as dark as the first one around the edges of the body, naturally laying in more on the shadowed side.

Immediately dip a medium-sized sable brush in a large jar of clean water; vigorously, but carefully, shake out most of the water and run the brush through the tint just laid, blending it into the basic flesh tone. Remember your water-bearing board and glycerine-treated color will help prevent quick-drying hard edges, permitting you to achieve a smooth subtle blending of colors. *Slowly*, keep building up color in this way, turning the board frequently to facilitate angling the brush into the area being painted, not out. Work in small sections—an arm, a leg—always turning the board to assure you freedom of movement.

It's better to build your color slowly rather than try to cope with too heavy a wash. I have, a number of times, taken a painting I felt was too thick with color and given it a warm shower. Experiment can produce some remarkable results.

You can't leave a damp board untended. If you are going to be away from your painting for any length of time, place a clean, smooth, nonabsorbent flat paper over the painting and over that place a heavy board. This will prevent curling. If on returning to your painting you feel it needs more color, *section* by *section* spread more of your basic light flesh tint over an entire area, quickly and carefully. Slowly build your color as you did originally.

When the flesh and hair are fully painted, it is time for details and props. On costuming and props never go directly to the darkest tone. Start as you did with the flesh. Use the lightest shade of gray even if the area is to be black. I use a number of accessory media for this: Mongol pencils applied with a blending stump (*never* use wax pencils!); Conti Carre's sanguine and brown chalks (very often I will lay in all basic modeling with these chalks using a blending stump, after my palest initial skin tone has been laid. My next washes of color are run right over the chalk, which isn't affected at all.); Koh.i.noor sepia leads #2633; and Grumbacher "Symphonie" watercolor tablets for lips, eyes. As for brushes, I use nothing but the very best sable—don't fool around with brushes! Watercolor is the easiest thing to work with if you *take your time* and *don't panic!*

Insofar as the airbrush is concerned there is little technical advice I can offer. You simply have to experiment with it, and above all don't let it rule you. The danger is in going hog-wild. It should only be used when a painting can be considered three-quarters finished or, better yet, totally finished. Don't try to make it do what *you* should have done with your watercolors and sable brushes. If you do, it will look mechanical and have no warmth. Because of the heavy demands on my time during my *Esquire* period, I leaned heavily on the airbrush. My recent work will often have none. Use it modestly, for subtle softness. It should *never* be obvious. I have never seen a good painting done entirely with airbrush. I use "frisket" to block out areas not to be painted. I

had never used frisket until I began working for *Esquire*. I was embarrassed to admit this, and it took me weeks to figure out how to work with it; but my favorite old friends are a group of random curved templates cut from a medium-weight very smooth paper. As I said, I have a number of these. By simply turning them I can match an edge to the curve of any part of the body. To achieve a soft edge I hold the template a ½ inch or so away from the area. To achieve a hard edge I hold it against the area. Used professionally and with utter discretion, the airbrush is a valid adjunct to a watercolor painting.

Finally, my continued admonition, don't rush your basic painting. Don't lay on your color too fast, build it gradually.

It can't hurt if you do this before beginning [Alberto crosses himself].

Alberto Vargas

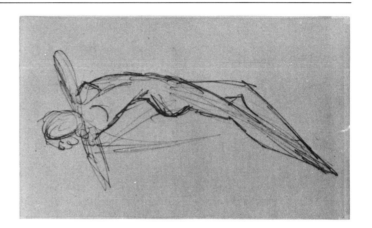

ACKNOWLEDGMENTS

This book is brought to you courtesy of World War II. Salutations for other more immediate contributions are in order.

First singular person to whom I owe love and gratitude is Alberto Vargas. An intelligent man, enthusiastic and erudite. A warm and modest man, who worked tirelessly; plucking rare and wonderful rabbits out of hats, offering sympathy and encouragement when the shoe should have been reversed. He had the good sense to marry a lovely lady who saved things and kept them in good order —this book is hers.

To Jim Camperos who through endless inextinguishable enthusiasm made miracles, unearthing things vital to this volume's success, organizing photo sessions et al., my admiration and respect.

John Kacere, Ivan Karp of O. K. Harris Gallery, Don Smith of Jantzen, Inc., Karl Bornstein of Miracle Gallery, Beverly and Ray Saks of the Art Couple, L. E. Wendt, Joe DeMartini, and Mr. and Mrs. Morris Lopkin were all very helpful in supplying exceedingly rare prints or original paintings.

To Hugh Hefner and Arthur Paul many thanks for many things. Others at Playboy *who offered generous help are Mildred Zimmerman, Barbara Hoffman, Rose Jennings, and Arlene Bouras. Nice People.*

Esquire's late, great Arnold Gingrich was thoroughly gracious, very enlightening, and to the point. Myron Davis was, telephonically, equally informative and direct.

Helpful along a rocky road: Michael Schau who acted as inadvertent catalyst and opened like a blossom giving much needed advice; Robert Baral for elegant atmosphere and accuracy; Doris Vinton of the Ziegfeld Club; Leroy Neiman, Astrid Conti, and Max Vargas for their devotion to Tio Alberto; most especially to Jo Ouelette, Lani Schoenke, and Shirley Uricho who made order out of my handwriting and offered innumerable valuable suggestions.

To my teachers at Norwich Art School (the best in the country) whose concerted disdain for things "Vargas" only fired an ever-increasing passion, my appreciation of their motives and my thanks.

A special dedication to Adelaide Christman Austin whose loving, liberal nature allowed her adolescent to spend nonexistent money on and plaster the walls with "Vargas" gatefolds and calendars; to her mother Grace Christman; to my father Herman Austin; and to Thure and Dorothy Dahl whose generosity ensured one nineteen-year-old's future.

Finally to Michael Turro who made it through the whole thing with patience and moral support above and beyond; Roger Weckerly whose unique character glued it together; and Miss Dee who, with them, listened to all the moans and groans.

Bless you all.